SCIENCE CONTENT FOR ELEMENTARY AND MIDDLE SCHOOL TEACHERS

PENELOPE FRITZER

Florida Atlantic University

VALERIE J. BRISTOR

Florida Atlantic University

PEARSON

Boston   New York   San Francisco   Mexico City
Montreal   Toronto   London   Madrid   Munich   Paris
Hong Kong   Singapore   Tokyo   Cape Town   Sydney

Series Editor: *Traci Mueller*
Marketing Manager: *Elizabeth Fogarty*
Editorial Assistant: *Krista E. Price*
Production Administrator: *Marissa Falco*
Editorial Production: *Omegatype Typography, Inc.*
Composition and Prepress Buyer: *Linda Cox*
Manufacturing Buyer: *Andrew Turso*
Cover Administrator: *Jill Winitzer*
Electronic Composition: *Omegatype Typography, Inc.*

For related titles and support materials, visit our online catalog at
www.ablongman.com.

Between the time Website information is gathered and then published, it is
not unusual for some sites to have closed. Also, the transcription of URLs can
result in unintended typographical errors. The publishers would appreciate
notification where these errors occur so that they may be corrected in
subsequent editions.

Fritzer, Penelope Joan.
    Science content for elementary and middle school teachers / Penelope
Fritzer, Valerie Bristor.
        p.   cm.
    Includes bibliographical references and index.
    ISBN 0-205-40798-6 (pbk.)
        1. Science—Study and teaching (Elementary)   2. Science—Study and
teaching (Middle school)   I. Bristor, Valerie.   II. Title.

LB1585.F75 2004
372.3′5—dc21

                                                                2003051827

Printed in the United States of America

10 9 8 7 6 5   07

This book is dedicated to
Bart Bland and Andrew Fritzer
and to
Ben and Joyce Bristor

Many thanks to Dr. Judith Covington, Dr. Deborah Jenkins, and Dr. Leticia Bridges, for their myriad prompt and helpful suggestions

Special thanks to Jennifer Bristor for her cheerful assistance

CONTENTS

PREFACE: A WORD TO THE READER

This book is a short primer in content to be used by the hard-pressed elementary or middle school science teacher as a quick reference to science concepts, events, influence, and chronology. Though it may not be all-inclusive or relevant for every grade level, this book is appropriate for any teacher wishing to be better informed and more confident about teaching science. Many states are strengthening their science content in the younger grades as part of the standards movement, and this book will help teachers gain the confidence to keep up with and to integrate newly required content.

For reasons of space, this book does not detail each state's requirements individually. Based broadly on the national standards, it gives the teacher enough general scientific information to cover most states' standards. It also provides a broad enough overview of how science and technology relate to the social context to allow the teacher to understand the scientific contribution to important events and inventions, to see where significant trends in human history fit scientifically, and to help in the teacher's own understanding of science concepts and events.

This is not a methods book. There are many good science methods books on the market that address, for example, interesting ways of students learning about the solar system, mussels, or chemical reactions. Rather, this book is aimed at raising the content knowledge of the teacher—often a problem with elementary education majors because the many pedagogy courses they must take frequently crowd out content courses. Science is often neglected at the elementary level, especially with the current emphasis on standardized testing of reading and math, but experience indicates that lack of teacher knowledge is also a major factor in the weakness of elementary science teaching.

Scientific illiteracy is rampant in the general public. Widespread lack of knowledge about the limits and practice of science leave many people having unrealistic expectations about what science can accomplish, as well as often viewing those who work in the field as "mad scientists." Additionally, due to a lack of scientific knowledge, much of the public has difficulty parsing out the meaning of scientific research reported in the popular press, often leading to either apathy or antagonism about new discoveries.

Scientific illiteracy in elementary teachers is a serious impairment to good science teaching. It is a truism that people teach what they know and are comfortable with, so teachers' lack of knowledge inhibits both their willingness to teach and their enthusiasm about science lessons. Elementary teachers (in most states this includes middle school grade six) do not need extensive in-depth knowledge about arcane scientific material—that can be left to those usually certified in science, teaching the upper grades. Rather, to successfully teach at the elementary and lower middle school level, teachers need a sound understanding of basic science principles, which this book will help provide.

Some states, such as Florida, have put science on required, standardized state tests in an effort to rectify the dismal state of science knowledge of many teachers and students. This gives teachers increased motivation to become more conversant with basic scientific knowledge and principles, so they can help their students succeed. This book is intended specifically to help address lack of teacher content knowledge in such situations.

Given that love of or distaste for science generally originates in elementary school, it is important that students develop scientific literacy to enable them to be thinking citizens who can grapple with the great scientific and moral questions of their time. As science increasingly advances into the realm of the previously unknown, questions about the regulation of issues such as cloning, researching stem cells, or disseminating personal medical information based on hereditary factors, become issues in the public discourse. For students to participate as thinking citizens and as voters, they should be prepared with basic scientific knowledge. They can then extrapolate that knowledge to reason intelligently about a wide variety of issues.

This book, in order to help fill the knowledge gap for elementary teachers, is organized into eight basic chapters: Why Study Science?; The History and Nature of Science; Biology; Ecology and the Environment; Earth and Oceans; Space, Weather and Climate; The Physical Sciences; and Science and Technology. There is also a substantial index, as well as lists of content resources.

We would like to acknowledge the following reviewers for their suggestions: Letitia Bridges, State University of West Georgia; and Jill A. Mizell, State University of West Georgia.

CHAPTER 1

WHY STUDY SCIENCE?

Most people are interested in their or their families' personal experiences and actions, and modern science has shaped many of those experiences and actions. Science is a manifestation of the desire for knowledge, and it extends to and influences local, national, and international experiences. Medicine, communications, travel, space exploration, labor-saving devices, entertainment, and a myriad of other endeavors are different for modern humans than in the past due to the scientific advances of the last few hundred years, and particularly of the twentieth century. As humankind enters the twenty-first century, science is increasingly important and influential, often advancing ahead of legal and ethical decision making.

Ideas and knowledge about our world, often in the realm of science, help make us truly and uniquely human. The importance of knowledge, and control and dissemination of that knowledge, has driven the development of increasingly scientific curricula in recent years and has resulted in vast differences and opportunities between those who move easily in the world of knowledge and those who struggle with it. Ideally, knowledge is far-reaching, democratic, and accessible to all. Hence, the importance of teachers knowledgeable about science content in every school, not just in affluent schools, which often offer higher pay and better working conditions.

Science is inseparable from humankind's activities—it has shaped and continues to shape people's experiences, knowledge, conflicts, diversions, diet, housing, and, indeed, every aspect of life. Science is even crucial when finding meaning in historical events, such as in the ongoing debate about the decision to drop the atomic bomb, a new scientific advance at the time, to end World War II. Science is morally neutral: the wonderful invention of the airplane was used by terrorists to kill thousands on September 11, 2001, but the creation of the smallpox and polio vaccines saved millions of lives. Similarly, the current anxiety about the possibility of biological warfare is a continuation of a problem that, on a more primitive scale, reaches back in history to the Great Plague of 1348 and even to the ancient Greeks' use of phosphorus as "Greek fire" against their enemies over 2,000 years ago.

Science is a path to understanding the world. Some major scientific questions that will affect most people's lives are: How long will you live? What kind of health will you be in? What kind of medical advances will be available to you and how do you want to die? What kind of labor will you do? What kind of fuel will you use? Will you wear natural fibers or man-made? Will you ride or walk? What kind of food will you eat and how will it be preserved? How will you entertain yourself? How will you communicate? How will your country defend itself, preserve natural resources, or get to outer space? The questions, like human interests, are endless. How they are answered matters greatly to all individuals, whether they realize it or not.

Most humans are affected by the advances, and occasional setbacks, of science. Much of the history of humankind is the history of dealing with people's relationship to science and with the way they, individually and in groups, live their lives. At the time of this writing, religious fundamentalists the world over are resisting, sometimes violently, the encroachment of modernity, often in the form of science. They are acting in a long tradition, since from time immemorial, people's lives have been and are inextricably intertwined with forms of science. Whether benevolent or militaristic, helpful or hindering, science affects not only the overall quality of life, but many other details of life and living for nearly every human being.

CHAPTER 2

THE HISTORY AND NATURE
OF SCIENCE

Science is the study of nature and nature's response to various stimuli. For example, one might study the make-up of clouds or clams, or what happens when cold air condenses in clouds, or when clams are exposed to pollution. The "pure" sciences like chemistry or biology provide the basis for the "applied" sciences like medicine, engineering, or even agriculture. Science has always been a part of the human experience to some degree or another, from the time when cave dwellers learned to create fire or to process animal hides.

For the last several hundred years, scientists, or people making scientific studies, have striven for "scientific method," a strict step-by-step method of setting up experiments or observations, trying to control for variables, or differences in results. For example, if one studies what happens when a chemical is heated, or when weed killer is used on crops, it is important that the experiments be controlled and that there not be other factors (than heat or weed killer, respectively) that could affect the result. One of the key elements of any experiment is controlling for various factors, known as "variables." It can be difficult to change just one condition while keeping the others constant. The person doing the weed killer experiment above, for example, might have trouble controlling the amount of rain that falls, insects that invade, or days of cloud cover—all of which are factors that could affect the results of the experiment.

The basis of the scientific method is recognizing the problem, which is generally done through observation. The next step is to form a hypothesis or educated guess about why the problem exists or what the solution might be. In order to do that, the scientist designs an experiment to test the hypothesis. The experiment is observed and the data, or information, is recorded. The records are kept in a careful fashion, known as the "protocol." The scientist hopes that the data, usually organized into tables or charts and analyzed statistically, will yield conclusions about whether the hypothesis is right or wrong. If more data is collected and analyzed, with the same results, the hypothesis is usually considered to be proven true. Even a hypothesis that does not prove to be true often adds to knowledge, as it allows researchers to eliminate some hypotheses.

Even non-scientists constantly theorize and test their theories, albeit mostly on a personal scale. For example, deciding why a cake didn't rise, then trying it again with more or less of a particular ingredient, or with a change in baking temperature, is a scientific experiment, as is trying several types of barbecue sauces or methods to get the juiciest chicken. When a person takes a particular cold medicine one day and another the next day, or paints two sections of a wall with two different types of paint, he or she is trying an experiment, controlled to a greater or lesser degree.

Science promotes observation, information, and experimentation. It repudiates superstition, guesswork, and blind tradition. Often people are uncomfortable with new information that scientists discover, but science is a neutral process of continually adding information to human knowledge—whether the general public welcomes that knowledge or not. It is sometimes very hard for people to adjust when science collides with tradition, so science is often in the news as decisions have to be made by society based on new scientific knowledge or achievements. Medical advances—such as in-vitro fertilization, organ transplants, or the right to die—are particular areas of contention, and they are also areas in which scientists are constantly re-evaluating their hypotheses and knowledge, based on new information and experiments.

MEASUREMENT

Measurement is a major part of science and the scientific method. The International System of Units, known as SI, is based on the metric system and used in most of the scientific world. Although it was adopted worldwide by the scientific community in 1960, the metric system was already in common use. The metric system was invented by French scientists in the 1600s, adopted by the revolutionary government in 1791, and imposed by Napoleon when he conquered much of Europe in the early 1800s—which is why it did not spread to unconquered Great Britain or the United States. But since Great Britain converted completely to the metric system in the 1970s, the United States is an oddity in that the metric system is in only very minor use here outside of the scientific community. This makes trade with the rest of the world somewhat more difficult than it should be, since most former European colonies in Africa, Asia, and Latin America have also adopted the metric system.

Metric measures are easy to handle, since they are based on powers of ten. All length measurements are pegged to the length of the meter, either larger (kilometer) or smaller (centimeters or millimeters), and in that relationship, they show the full power to the metric system. The rough guide for those unfamiliar with the metric system is that a meter is a little longer than a yard, an inch is about 2 and a half centimeters, and a kilometer is roughly 6/10 of a mile. "Milli" is the prefix meaning "one-thousandth," "centi" is the prefix meaning "one-hundredth," and "deci" is the prefix meaning "one-tenth." Additionally, "kilo" is the prefix meaning "one thousand," "hecto" is the prefix for "one hundred," and "deka" is the prefix for "ten."

These prefixes are true for meters (length), grams (weight), and liters (volume), and, once familiar, they make the metric system easy to use. In addition, kilograms measure mass, which is different from weight. Mass is the amount of matter in an object, which never changes, while weight is a measurement of gravity, which can change depending on where the object is (for example, on the moon, where its weight would be lighter than on earth). There is no real need to memorize conversions or to practice the tasks of conversion between the traditional U.S. system and the metric system, as long as one understands how each is set up.

In measuring temperature, the scientific community uses the Kelvin scale. The Kelvin scale measures much as the widely used Celsius scale does, but zero degrees on the Kelvin scale, also known as "absolute zero," is the coldest temperature possible in nature. That is much colder than zero degrees on the Celsius scale, in which zero degrees equals the freezing point, and 100 degrees equals the boiling point of water. However, the general public in the United States uses Fahrenheit measurements, which put the temperature of freezing water at 32 degrees and boiling water at 212 degrees.

HISTORY

Science and the natural world have always existed, although it is mainly in the last few hundred years that people have attempted to codify and organize their knowledge of such subjects. Early attempts to explain the natural world were often based on superstition, magic, oversimplifying, or lack of observation—like the medieval idea that the body was composed of four "humors" (blood, phlegm, black bile, and yellow bile). Science has become such an important part of most civilizations that most of us cannot imagine our world without it. We often see and interpret the world based on our familiarity with scientific knowledge.

Early humans observed and discovered scientific truths. They tracked the phases of the moon, for example, and learned that the tides were linked to those phases, and they established ways of predicting the seasons and of telling approximate time. Science has been practiced by nearly everyone and is itself as old as human history. Early humankind, through trial and error, developed the ability to make fire, to do metalworking, to use the wheel, and to practice agriculture—all major scientific advancements. It is thought that even the most ancient societies had some forms of science, and science is found in writings as far back as the ancient civilizations of the Sumerians, the Egyptians, the Chinese, and the Greeks. Body preservation, seafaring, irrigation, weaponry, improved agriculture, primitive medicine, timekeeping, and many other scientific innovations were all developed by various ancient cultures.

The Middle Ages in western Europe gave rise to the "sciences" of alchemy (trying to turn base metals into gold) and astrology (the forerunner of astronomy). Later, with the creation of scientific method, serious study of alchemy and astrology became chemistry and astronomy, as people gave up the idea of creating gold and reading behavior in the stars (except as entertainment). Improvements in navigation, beginning in the Middle Ages, included a better compass, and first the cross-staff, and then the back-staff, for measuring latitude (although an accurate way to measure longitude, the marine clock was not invented until 1761). These improvements led to greater exploration, and Europeans were able to colonize many parts of the world in the 1500s and 1600s also because of the nearly simultaneous invention of the gun.

In the 1500s, Francis Bacon noted that "Good science is useful science," and promoted scientific methods of observation. From approximately that time onward, many great scientific discoveries were made, especially in physics, and especially during the 1600s and 1700s, in the period known as the Enlightenment. Copernicus suggested a sun-centered solar system (instead of an earth-centered one); Galileo promoted that theory and performed scientific experiments with telescopes and with the rate at which items fall; Tycho Brahe kept extensive records of his astronomical observations and theorized that the planets revolved in circles; Johannes Kepler (building on Brahe's observations) discovered that the planets revolved in ellipses, rather than in circles; and Isaac Newton not only invented calculus but also published a very significant book explaining the laws of gravity and motion.

In 1774, Joseph Priestly determined that air was a mixture of gases, and was able to isolate oxygen. Antoine Lavoisier built on Priestly's work to make the first table of chemical elements, and is considered to have founded modern chemistry. In the early 1800s, John Dalton originated an early version of atomic theory (the ancient Greek, Democritus, had proposed a more primitive version even before the time of Christ), and later Dmitri Mendeleev made a well-received table of the elements. In the late 1800s, Wilhelm Roentgen discovered X-rays (the X stood for "unknown"), and Marie and Pierre Curie worked with radiation, first discovered by A. H. Bequerel.

The Industrial Revolution first began in England in the early 1700s and spread throughout the 1800s in what came to be known as the "industrialized world." Some of the early inventions that give the period its name are: an engine to pump water out of coal mines; a mechanical drill that allowed faster planting; and the flying shuttle and the spinning jenny which contributed to faster weaving of cloth and making of thread. In the United States, Eli Whitney invented the cotton gin, which picked the seeds out of cotton fibers. This invention greatly increased the manufacturing of cloth and led to the increased use of slave labor to grow cotton in the South.

Many other scientific advances were also made during the Industrial Revolution, including new, more efficient ways of making iron and steel, which led to more efficient weapons and to the invention of the steam ship, the railroad, and the first (relatively low) skyscrapers. The new heavy equipment led to the widespread digging of canals and use of barges for transporting goods. Other innovations of the period included the electric battery (invented by Alessandro Volta) and generator (Michael Faraday), the telegraph (Samuel Morse), the telephone (Alexander Graham Bell), the radio (Guglielmo Marconi), and the light bulb and record player (Thomas Edison, who invented many other things as well).

The 1800s, with their widespread exploration and colonization of other parts of the world by Europe, also were the time of the rapid rise of biology, partly as a result of the Europeans finding many unfamiliar plants and animals. Early in the century, J. B. Lamarck, from observations of fossils, suggested that living things change gradually to adapt to their environment. Charles Darwin (evolution), Alfred Wallace (evolution), and Gregor Mendel (genetics) continued to work along those lines. Exploration also helped establish the science of geology. Its foundation, laid in the 1700s by James Hutton, who suggested the earth was constantly changing, was further established in the 1800s by Charles Lyell, who wrote about the physical history and make-up of the earth.

Despite all of this scientific activity, the modern idea of science as an academic subject is relatively recent. One of the great changes in higher education in the European and British universities in the late 1800s (called the nineteenth century, as the first century starts with the year 1 and the second century starts with the year 100, so the number of the century never matches the number of the year) was the incorporation of science as a respectable academic subject. This trend was begun by the Germans and particularly highlighted by the career of the Englishman Thomas Huxley (called "Darwin's Bulldog" for defending evolution) who, like Darwin, got his start as a ship's surgeon, not as an academic. Huxley carried the battle of science education forward, being largely responsible for Cambridge and Oxford's shift from exclusively classical education to inclusion of modern science subjects, with their consequent influence on other universities.

By the 1900s, the first motion pictures and automobiles were becoming common, and Henry Ford put together his assembly line for building cars in 1914. In 1903, the Wright brothers flew the first motor-powered plane. The list of scientific, medical and technological inventions of the twentieth century is endless, but some of the most influential and widespread are automobiles, television, flight and space travel, atomic power, computers, and improvements in sanitation, communications, weapons, and medicine (including antibiotics and birth control).

The twentieth century is known for discoveries in physics, which contributed to many inventions, particularly in atomic power, weaponry, and space travel. In 1905, Albert Einstein published his "theory of relativity," which dealt with the nature of matter moving near the speed of light, and suggested that mass and energy can be converted into each other. Early in the century, J. J. Thomson discovered the electron, Ernest Rutherford and Niels Bohr suggested models of the atom, and Max Planck identified short bursts of energy, called "quanta."

From the Industrial Revolution onward, more and more nations have adopted the advances of modern science, and it has spread around the world, improving the average life span and standard of living. In a world increasingly connected by technological invention, science has its negative side, as well, mostly in relation to the danger of nuclear and biological weapons, and of degradation of the environment through pollution and overpopulation.

READINGS FOR STUDENTS

Adler, D. (1999). *A Picture Book of George Washington Carver.* New York: Holiday House.

Anderson, M. (1997). *Isaac Newton: The Greatest Scientist of All Time.* Berkley Heights: Enslow.

Batten, M. (2001). *Anthropologist: Scientist of the People.* Boston: Houghton Mifflin.

Castner, J. (2001). *Rainforest Researchers.* Salt Lake City: Benchmark Books/Marshall Cavendish.

DuTemple, L. (2000). *Jacques Cousteau.* Minneapolis: Lerner Publications.

Holmes, T. (1998). *Fossil Fuel: The Rivalry of the First American Dinosaur Hunters.* New York: Messner.

Jackson, D. (1997). *The Bone Detectives: How Forensic Anthropologists Solve Crimes and Uncover Mysteries of the Dead.* Boston: Little, Brown.

January, B. (1999). *Science in the Renaissance* (Science of the Past Series). London: Franklin Watts/Grolier.

Kahl, J. (1997). *Weather Watch: Forecasting the Weather.* Minneapolis: Lerner.

Kramer, S. (2001). *Hidden Worlds: Looking Through a Scientist's Microscope.* Boston: Houghton Mifflin.

McCaffrey, C. (2001). *The Head Bone's Connected to the Neck Bone: The Weird, Wacky, and Wonderful X-ray.* New York: Farrar, Straus and Giroux.

McPherson, S. (2001). *Jonas Salk: Conquering Polio.* Minneapolis: Lerner Publications.

McPherson, S. (1996). *Ordinary Genius: The Story of Albert Einstein.* Minneapolis: Carolrhoda.

Patent, D. (2001). *Charles Darwin: The Life of a Revolutionary Thinker.* New York: Holiday House.

Pemberton, D. (2001). *Egyptian Mummies: People from the Past.* San Diego: Harcourt's Children's Books.

Relf, P. (2000). *A Dinosaur Named Sue: The Story of the Colossal Fossil.* New York: Scholastic.

Seibert, P. (1999). *Discovering El Nino: How Fable and Fact Together Help Explain the Weather.* Brookfield, CT: Millbrook Press.

Stanley, P. (1997). *American Environmental Heroes.* Berkley Heights: Enslow.

Thimmesh, C. (2000). *Girls Think of Everything: Stories of Ingenious Inventions by Women.* Boston: Houghton Mifflin.

Van Meter, V. and Gutman, D. (1996). *Taking Flight.* New York: Viking.

Vanderwarker, P. (2001). *The Big Dig: Reshaping an American City.* Boston: Little, Brown.

Webster, S. (2000). *The Kingfisher Book of Evolution.* Boston: Kingfisher.

Wilson, A. (1999). *How the Future Began: Communications.* New York: Kingfisher.

Yount, L. (1997). *Anton van Leeuwenhoek: First to See Microscopic Life.* Berkley Heights: Enslow.

WEBSITES

National Science Teacher Association
www.nsta.org

Lesson Plans
www.theteacherscorner.net/science/miscellaneous/index.htm

Science Topics
place.scholastic.com/magicschoolbus/home.htm

Mini-lessons/elementary
ofcn.org/cyber.serv/academy/ace/sci/elem.html

Mini-lessons/intermediate
ofcn.org/cyber.serv/academy/ace/sci/inter.html

Lesson Plans, Maps, Online Adventures
www.nationalgeographic.com/education/index.html

Lesson Plans
www.lessonplanspage.com/Science.htm

Science Topics
www.EnchantedLearning.com/Home.html

Variety of Topics
www.adprima.com/mainmenu.htm

Reading Rainbow
gpn.unl.edu/rainbow

Science Projects Ideas
www.isd77.k12.mn.us/resources/cf/SciProjIntro.html
www.nsta.org/213 Outstanding Science Tradebooks for Children 1996–2001

Science Ideas for Children
www.nsta.org/211
www.nsta.org/212
www.nsta.org/214
www.nsta.org/215
www.nsta.org/216

Evolution
www.napedu/readingroom/books/evolution98/contents.html
www.nsta.org/342
www.nsta.org/340
www.indiana.edu/~ensiweb/home.html

Denver Museum of Nature and Science
www.dmnh.org/

Online Science
www.project2061.org/tools/sfaaol/Chap1.htm#Nature

Nature and Philosophy of Science
www.angelfire.com/mn2/tisthammerw/science.html

Science Education
psci-com.org/uk/browse/ypages/507.html

Teaching History and Nature of Science
www.thebakken.org/education/SciMathMN/teaching-history-and-nature-of-science.htm

Science Netlinks
www.sciencenetlinks.com/

Education at the National Academies
www.nas.edu/subjectindex/edu.html

Nature of Science—Scientific Method Main Concepts
www.quia.com/jg/65726.html

Nature of Science
www.chemsoc.org/networks/learnnet/nature.htm

Science Links
www/literacynet.org/sciencelincs/slhistory.html

■ ■ ■ ■ ■

CHAPTER 3

BIOLOGY

The earth is made up of both living and non-living things, and the study of living things, called "organisms," is known as biology (from the Greek "bio" meaning "life" and "ology" meaning "study" or "body of knowledge"). Within biology's various scientific subjects, there are many different categories. The two main areas of biology are zoology (the study of animals and derived from the word "zoo") and botany (the study of plants and the root for the word "botanical"). Although biology is a subject that was studied as far back as 500 B.C. in ancient Greece, the term "biology" has only been common in English since the early 1800s, when Sir William Lawrence published his book *On the Physiology, Zoology, and Natural History of Man.*

As the earth formed, matured, and aged, so did the life that appeared on it. In the Precambrian Era, ranging from about 4 billion years ago to about 600 million years ago, the earth's crust was formed and primitive life first appeared. Next, in the Paleozoic Era, trilobites (simple marine invertebrates with three-part bodies) and brachiopods (mollusk-like marine animals) were a common form of life at first. Then simple land plants, fish, corals, amphibians, and reptiles appeared, respectively, and coal began to form out of the carbon from decomposed plant and animal life. In the next period, the Mesozoic Era, dinosaurs were dominant, and birds and mammals appeared, along with plants which produced flowers, fruit, and seed. Finally, in the Cenozoic Era, which includes the present time, dinosaurs disappeared, mammals (including humans) became abundant, and many kinds of plant and animal life flourished.

The ancient Greeks' quest for knowledge led them to examine living things as well as to explore various other subjects such as mathematics and drama. Two of the most famous Greek scientists, Hippocrates and Aristotle, concentrated on anatomy and physiology, the study of the make-up of the body. Hippocrates laid the foundation of modern medicine and his "Hippocratic Oath," beginning "First, do no harm...," is still sworn to by most doctors when they graduate from medical school. In about 350 B.C. Aristotle divided plants and animals into categories and made many careful observations of the human body, including trying to examine the relationship of the soul or "psyche" to the body. Both Hippocrates and Aristotle, as well as other Greek scientists, were involved in trying to classify various kinds of animals and plants, as was Pliny, a Roman. Galen was a later Greek scientist who harkened back to Hippocrates and Aristotle with his studies on the body, particularly on the spinal cord, but when he died about 200 A.D, no one carried on his work.

The various independent Greek states were conquered by the Roman Empire, but after the fall of that empire in A.D. 476, Europe entered a time of limited scientific learning. The most important step for biology in that period was the translation of Aristotle's works into Latin—the international language of medieval scholars. Knowledge in general benefitted from the growing interaction with the Byzantine Empire and the Arabic world. By the late 1400s, during the Renaissance, many artists such as Michelangelo Buonarroti and Leonardo da Vinci had turned their attention to botanical drawings and to detailed studies of the human body—helped along in da Vinci's case by human dissection. By the 1500s and 1600s, the movement toward botanical and zoological knowledge grew strong all over Europe, especially with the publication in Switzerland of Konrad von Gesner's five volume, comprehensive study of animals.

The new interest in botany and zoology coincided with the Age of Exploration—when Europeans traversed the globe to the so-called New World, as well as around Africa and into Asia and the Pacific. These explorations provided constant new discoveries for botanists and zoologists. Tomatoes, potatoes, blueberries, chocolate, and tobacco were some of the botanical items brought from the New World to Europe for the first time in the 1500s, while sugar, cotton, silk, and various spices were imported from Africa and Asia. Similarly, the first European "zoos" were built, as "exotic" African, Indian, and American animals were brought to Europe.

In 1628, a major step forward in biology came when William Harvey published his work explaining the circulation of the blood. As the century continued, Robert Hooke and Anton van Leeuwenhoek made many valuable observations about plant and animal life using the newly invented microscopes. Beginning with Aristotle, many early scholars had created ways of organizing plant and animal life. The most successful and long-lasting system was that originated by the Swedish scientist Carl von Linne (*Carolus Linnaeus* in Latin) in the 1700s, and, with some alterations, it is still used today.

In the 1700s, explorers such as Captain Cook, who explored the Pacific Northwest and Polynesia, deliberately took naturalists with them on overseas voyages. By the mid-1800s, Charles Darwin was sailing on the *Beagle* to the Galapagos Islands, where he made the observations that led to his theory of evolution, published in 1859 (an idea that was also postulated by Alfred Russell Wallace). In 1872, the British sent the ship *Challenger* on a well-organized voyage of scientific exploration, which reported important information about various subjects, including oceanography, botany, and zoology.

The 1800s were years of great advancement in all kinds of scientific studies. In the early 1800s, John James Audubon created the detailed paintings presented in his folios *The Birds of America* and *The Quadrupeds of America*. In the 1830s, two Germans, Matthias Schleiden and Theodor Schwann, discovered cells in plant life and animals, leading them to the idea that all living things are made up of cells. Another important scientist of the period was Louis Agassiz, Swiss naturalist and Harvard professor, who pioneered the idea of studying animals in their natural surroundings. In 1866, the Austrian monk Gregor Mendel determined the laws of heredity by breeding, observing, and documenting the characteristics of pea plants. A few years later, the Frenchman Louis Pasteur discovered that germs cause disease (the pasteurization of milk to kill bacteria takes its name from him). The American Luther Burbank performed many experiments in plant hybridization (or cross-breeding), creating new forms of fruit, grasses, flowers, grains, and vegetables.

The twentieth century brought many new innovations in biology. Some of the most significant advancements occurred in the area of medicine, and include the discoveries of penicillin and DNA (deoxyribonucleic acid), the ability to do organ transplants, and the mapping of the human genome. Another important movement, ecology, began attracting attention in the 1960s. Ecology studies the interconnectedness of all things in nature, and attempts to balance human needs with preserving the environment and various plants and animals, some on the brink of extinction.

CLASSIFICATION

Classification of knowledge into categories is called "taxonomy," and the taxonomy of biology (mainly plants and animals) was originally attempted by Aristotle in ancient Greece. The system currently in use is based, as noted, on Linnaeus's system. While Linnaeus used four categories (class, order, genus, species), modern plant and animal taxonomy uses several more (kingdom, phylum, class, order, family, genus, species). The modern system, however, sticks to Linnaeus's binomial system of nomenclature, which uses two ("bi") Latin words for each name ("nomenclature"), the first word being the genus name and the second word being the species name. Usually, each name is descriptive of the plant or animal, making the system quite simple, although it may seem very complex at first. Linnaeus chose Latin because that was still the international language of scholars when he was writing in the early 1700s.

The levels of classification are kingdom, phylum, class, order, family, genus, and species. "Kingdom" refers to the most general category of the item being studied. Although for many years there were considered to be only two kingdoms, plant and animal, now scientists believe there are six (some scientists lump the two bacteria kingdoms together and call them monerans, which leaves only five kingdoms) and there may be more identified in coming years.

1. Animals—many celled, feed on other living things.
2. Plants—many celled, make their own food.
3. Fungi—single or many-celled, with a nucleus, but cannot make their own food, as plants do.
4. Protists—single or many-celled with a nucleus, some make their own food, some do not.
5. Eubacteria—single-celled, some make their own food, some do not.
6. Archaebacteria—single-celled, no nucleus, some make their own food, some do not.

The next distinction, "phylum" (called "division" in botany), is also the next largest group. Each phylum is divided into "classes," which refer to the most common qualities of members of a phylum. For example, a member of the animal kingdom might be labelled in the phylum *chordata* (subphylum *vertebrata*) and in the class *mammalia*, because animals in this class nurse their young. In the next distinction, these mammals belong to one of several different "orders," depending, for example, upon whether the mammals have hooves (*Ungulata*), like cows, or are flesh-eating (*Carnivora*), like tigers or wolves. The order is made up of related "families," a family such as *Canidae* (the dog family) being made up of closely related groups, called *Genera* (the plural of *Genus*), like domestic dogs, coyotes, and wolves. *Genus,* in turn, refers to a group of closely related "species" (a group of very similar organisms with common ancestors), while a "variety," or "sub-species" may differ slightly from others within the species, but not enough to be a separate species.

This all may seem quite complicated, but, in fact, it is a very organized system, and familiarity with it makes information easy to grasp. Continuing with the dog example, a St. Bernard would be a member of the kingdom *animalia,* the phylum *chordata* (in the subphylum *vertebrata*), the class *mammalia,* the order *carnivora,* the family *canidae,* the genus *canis,* the species *domesticus,* and the variety St. Bernard.

KINGDOMS

Fungi, formerly thought to be plants, are now considered a kingdom. Like plants, they grow in soil and have cell walls, but they do not make their own food as plants do, although they are similar in make-up. Most fungi feed on dead or decaying tissues and reproduce by spores—reproductive cells that form new organisms without fertilization. The most common fungi probably are mushrooms and yeast (which makes bread rise). Other common fungi create mold or cause diseases such as athlete's foot, and thrive in warm, damp environments.

Protists are another kingdom, and they are either single or many-celled organisms that have a nucleus. They vary widely, and can be plant-like (algae), animal-like (protozoans), or fungus-like (slime molds, water molds, white rusts, and downy mildews, such as that which caused the Irish potato blight and resulting famine).

The other two kingdoms are both bacteria, and there are many kinds of bacteria, including many beneficial ones that live in and on the human body. Although bacteria can cause disease, most do not. Cheese and yogurt are two examples of foods made with a culture of harmless bacteria. Other bacteria are valuable for processing nitrogen to enrich soil, for making medicines, and for eating up oil spills ("bioremediation," or using living organisms to change pollutants into harmless compounds).

The two kingdoms of bacteria are eubacteria (some of which contain chlorophyll to enable them to make their own food, but most do not) and archaebacteria (which usually live in extreme environments and may or may not make their own food). Eubacteria is a very diverse group and contains almost all kinds of bacteria. It is by far the largest of the two bacteria kingdoms. Archaebacteria contains some anaerobic bacteria, probably left over from the early years of earth's formation, that live in extreme conditions such as deep under water, in hot springs, or in places like the Dead Sea. The term "anaerobic" describes an organism that doesn't use oxygen to breath (an organism that does use oxygen to breathe is called an "aerobe").

Plants

Plants are one of the two major kingdoms. Plants are perhaps more important to life on earth than any other living things, as they produce both food and oxygen for themselves and other organisms. Plants are made of cell walls which provide structure and protection, and most (but not all) plants contain chlorophyll and have roots. Plants grow in almost all parts of the world, and range in size from tiny seedlings to giant redwood trees. Although there are over a quarter of a million identified plants, it is thought that there are actually many more in existence. Plants need air, light, water, nutrients, and minerals to grow and to make their own food. As the food source for most other living things, plants are major producers of energy: besides plants supporting themselves, most animals eat plants, and some animals eat other animals that eat plants. Although most living things need air to breathe and live, it has only been a little over 200 years that people were able to isolate oxygen and connect the idea of oxygen with the idea of photosynthesis—the process vital to most life by which plants produce oxygen from sunlight and carbon dioxide.

Plants are also important for helping to create and renew soil. Bacteria in the soil and on the roots of certain plants change the nitrogen content located there. The "nitrogen cycle" refers to plants making protein from nitrogen in the soil by changing it into nitrates and ammonia. Solid waste contains nitrates, urine contains ammonia, and dead organisms release nitrates and ammonia from decaying protein. Additionally, plants are used for food, fiber, medicine, paper, furniture, shelter, instruments, perfume, etc.

Plant life is very old, with fossils found from over 400 million years ago. Since plants use carbon dioxide and sunlight for the process of making food, which gives off oxygen, the amount of oxygen on earth grew as the amount of plants increased, making a more welcoming environment for those organisms that depend on oxygen. It is thought that plants may have evolved from the green algae branch of protists, and adapted to dry land with cell walls made of cellulose, which help reduce water loss. There are many adaptations plants make to various stimuli. A plant's response to stimulus is called a "tropism," so responding to light is called "phototropism," and responding to gravity is called "gravitropism." The Venus fly trap responds to stimulus of touch by closing on insects, some ferns respond to touch by curling up, and other plants respond to light by blooming only during day or night.

Plants, like animals, are divided into phyla (called "divisions" when dealing with plants), but other, practical categories are vascular and nonvascular. Vascular plants have tissues that make up their organ system and carry water and nutrients through the plant, while nonvascular plants have no vascular tissues, so move water and substances in other ways.

The most primitive plants are seedless and nonvascular, and they include liverworts and mosses, known together as "bryophytes." They are very small, with thread-like roots called "rhizoids." Water is absorbed and distributed directly through the cell walls of bryophytes, and they do not have seeds, but, rather, reproduce by spores. Because they are relatively hardy, bryophytes are often pioneer plants, the first to grow in a harsh environment such as a lava field.

Seedless vascular plants also reproduce by spores, but they have vascular tissue with cells to carry water and nutrients. They include ground pines, spike mosses, horsetails, and ferns—all small plants, although fossils show that some used to be much bigger. Many abundant early plants decayed and compressed over millions of years to form the basis for fossil fuels such as coal.

Seed plants are much more sophisticated, as they have roots, stems, leaves, and vascular tissue, and they produce stored food in the form of seeds, which are the source of energy not only for the plant embryo, but for many animals as well. Angiosperms and gymnosperms are the two major groups of seed plants. Angiosperms refer to plants with broad leaves, and gymnosperms refer to plants with needles—which are mostly conifers and cacti.

Angiosperms are by far the bigger group, they vary greatly, and they are very important in feeding most animals, including humans. Angiosperms are all vascular plants that flower and have fruit that contains seeds, although some of the flowers are very subtle and hard to recognize as flowers. Angiosperms can be either monocotyledons ("mono" meaning one) or dicotyledons ("di" meaning two), known in short form as "monocots" or "dicots." Their names indicate that monocots have one seed leaf inside a seed, while dicots have two such seed leaves.

Gymnosperms are vascular plants that produce uncovered seeds, usually in cones, without fruit or flowers. Most gymnosperms are evergreens with needlelike leaves. The exception is the ginkgo, one of the oldest kinds of trees known, which has broad leaves that drop in the fall, unlike most gymnosperms.

Most seed plants have two or three kinds of vascular tissue: xylem (tubes that transport liquids from the roots throughout the plant), phloem (which moves food through the plant to be used or stored), and sometimes cambium (which produces new xylem and phloem cells).

Stems hold up plants, move water and allow movement of material between leaves and roots. They can be small and light (herbaceous, as with many flowers and vegetables) or large and heavy (woody, as with most trees and shrubs). Plants with soft, flexible stems usually are small and often live only one season. By contrast, those with stiff, woody stems and bark usually live many years. Stems often store food, and can be above ground, as with sugar cane, or underground, as with potatoes.

Most plants have roots, and root systems are sometimes the largest parts of plants. Roots generally grow underground and they are important not only for taking in, absorbing, and holding water and nutrients, but for anchoring and holding plants in soil, particularly on uneven or sloping ground. They are also vital for storing food (such as carrots). Some plants have a single tap root (one main root), and others have fibrous roots (many roots the same size). All roots have tiny "root hairs" to take in the needed water and nutrients.

Leaves come in many sizes, shapes, and colors. They take in light and make food, a process known as "photosynthesis." Most leaves have symmetry—each half is a mirror image of the other. A leaf is made of different layers of cells, and on the surfaces is the "epidermis," a thin layer of cells that covers and protects the leaf. The epidermis also has a cover, the "cuticle," which is a waxy substance that reduces evaporation.

"Stomata" are pores in the leaf surfaces—tiny holes for breathing and water escape. When plants breathe, stomata take in carbon dioxide and water and they give off oxygen, which is used by animals and humans. Stomata also let out water, taken in through the roots, as vapor (the giving off of water vapor from a plant is called "transpiration"). The stomata are usually open during the day and closed at night.

The inner parts of the leaf, between the epidermis on the top and bottom, are the palisade layer and the spongy layer. The palisade layer contains "chloroplasts" (cells that hold chlorophyll), and it makes food, while the spongy layer contains the "xylem" and "phloem," which transport the liquid and food.

A plant produces food when light energy is changed into chemical energy that is stored in sugar molecules. The chlorophyll traps the light energy, which splits water molecules and joins hydrogen from the water to carbon dioxide to form glucose sugar. The glucose gives the plant energy (food) for growth. Plants also make oxygen, and most of the oxygen is released through the leaves (the rest is used to break down food molecules and release their energy for growth and reproduction). This whole process by which plants make food and oxygen—photosynthesis—is common to most plants, but not all, and it is the reason why plants grow toward light ("photopropism"). In addition to light, water, and carbon dioxide, plants also need nutrients and minerals to thrive and make flowers and seeds.

Chlorophyll gives many plants their green color. Most leaves have so much green pigment from the chlorophyll that it hides other colors, but when the weather gets cold, the chlorophyll in some leaves breaks down, so the other pigments are seen as the leaves change color. Drought resistant plants often have gray or white leaves or bark that reflect sun, narrow leaves with waxy coating that keeps in moisture, and underground bulbs that are enlarged systems for storing food.

Animals

Animals are many-celled organisms that can move around, digest food, get rid of wastes, and reproduce. They need air, water, food, and habitat. They cannot make their own food, so they eat plants and/or other animals. Since all animals need oxygen, land animals get it from air, and water animals get it from water or surfacing for air, such as whales. The bodies of all animals contain a lot of water, which is usually replaced by drinking. Most animals also need shelter, which is often provided by plants, and animals often carry seeds, enrich soil, and pollinate. Animals, like plants, provide much food and many products for humans.

Trilobites, now extinct, were three to four inch long creatures that lived in the oceans billions of years ago and are thought to be some of the first animals. Currently, there are more than one and a half million kinds of animals, in addition to all those, such as dinosaurs, that are extinct. Aristotle was one of the first to try to classify animals. He divided them into two groups—those with backbones and red blood, and all others. Today, they are divided into two major groups—vertebrates (those with a backbone, including fish, birds, amphibians, reptiles, and mammals), which belong to the phylum *chordata*, and invertebrates (those without a backbone), which are spread over eight other phyla. Most animals have either radial symmetry (body parts arranged around a central point) or bilateral symmetry (matching sides of the body), although a few are asymmetrical (with no definite shape).

About 75 percent of all animals are insects, and the invertebrates in general, largely arthropods (including insects, spiders, crustaceans, and others), sponges, worms, and mollusks (hard shelled animals, like clams, and some without hard shells, like squid), together make up about 97 percent of all animals. Some invertebrates, such as worms and sponges, are completely soft, but many of the arthropods have "exoskeletons"—strong body armor that protects them and keeps them from drying out. Arthropods have multiple legs and often three body joints. Insects are arthropods, with six legs, as are spiders, with eight legs. Arthropods lay eggs, and many have four wings. Many insects, like butterflies, change form, beginning as eggs, developing into pupa (larvae), and becoming adults—each stage with its own distinct physical form.

The phylum *chordata* (which denotes animals with a rod of stiffened tissue and a hollow nerve cord in the back) contains the following three subphylum: tunicates, which have a sac-like body enclosed in a thick membrane known as a "tunic" which has two openings for water to enter and exit; lancelets, which are small, fishlike creatures with slender bodies pointed at each end and containing a rod-like cord of cells; and vertebrates, those animals having a segmented spinal column and a brain enclosed in a skull.

Vertebrates are considered the most physically sophisticated animals, in their phylum and overall. They include mammals, birds, reptiles, amphibians, and fish, but together vertebrates make up only about 3 percent of existing animals. Vertebrates have endoskeletons—skeletons within their skin—with bones that hold their muscles and support and protect their internal organs. Most vertebrates are ectotherms, whose body temperature changes with the temperature of their surroundings. The rest, including humans, are endotherms with constant body temperatures. Vertebrates include fish (scales and gills), amphibians (smooth wet skin), reptiles (dry, rough skin), birds (wings, two feet, feathers), and mammals (feed their young milk).

Fish, which are ectotherms, are the biggest group of vertebrates. Fish live in water, most have gills and scales, and they mostly reproduce by laying eggs. They use gills to get oxygen from the water, and they have fins for movement, balance, and steering. Their protective scales are thin bony plates covering their skin, and most scales are covered with slippery mucus that lets the fish slide easily through water. There are three classes of fish, bony, jawless, and cartilaginous.

The vast majority of fish are bony fish, which have skeletons made of bone, while the others have skeletons of cartilage, which is similar to bone but more flexible. Bony fish contain an air sac (known as the swim bladder) that helps the fish rise or fall in the water, depending on the amount of oxygen or nitrogen in the sac. Bony fish reproduce by the female laying eggs, then the males releasing sperm as they swim over the eggs.

Jawless fish, like lampreys, have round mouths with no jaws, and their mouths act as suckers so they can feed on larger fish. Although jawless fish also are cartilaginous fish—with skeletons made of cartilage—the rest of the cartilaginous fish, such as sharks, do have moveable jaws, and they have scales that feel like sandpaper. Sharks have cartilage instead of bones.

Amphibians, such as frogs, are also ectotherms—their body temperature changes with their environment—that live partly in water and partly on land. They reproduce by laying eggs in water, and they hibernate in the winter, or, if they live in hot, dry environments, they hide in the ground during summer, a form of inactivity called "estivation." Amphibians change from using gills to obtain oxygen when they are larvae—hatchlings from eggs—to using lungs to obtain it when they are fully developed, since in the larval stage, they live in the water, and in the adult stage, they live mostly on land. Amphibians begin life in water and move to land. Frogs, for example, begin life as eggs, become tadpoles with gills, and grow lungs as adults.

Reptiles are also ectotherms, and they have thick, dry, scaly, waterproof skin, and breathe with lungs. Reptiles are land animals that vary greatly in size, shape, and color. The three main types of reptiles are alligators and crocodiles, tortoises (land) and turtles (water), and snakes and lizards, with the snakes and lizards group being the largest. Unlike amphibians, reptiles reproduce with internal fertilization—in which sperm are deposited directly into the female's body—so fertilization is much more efficient than with amphibians. Reptile eggs, laid on land, have tough, leather-like coverings that provide protection until the young, fully-developed reptiles hatch, although some reptiles give birth to live young rather than laying eggs. Dinosaurs, now extinct, were reptiles, and the word "dinosaur" means "terrible lizard." There were many kinds of dinosaurs—including Triceratops, Tyrannosaurus Rex, Stegosaurus, Diplodocus, and Apatosaurus—which differed mainly by teeth, diet, and skin.

Birds are vertebrates that are endotherms—with constant body temperature—and each bird has feathers, wings, lungs, a beak, and two legs. Birds lay hard-shelled eggs and often sit on the eggs to keep them warm until they hatch, and they usually care for their young after hatching. Birds are classified into orders based on their feathers, beak shape, foot shape, and habits (wading birds like ibis, for example, often have long beaks and legs). Ability to fly, webbing of feet and shape of toes, and shape of beaks for catching food, all affect where and how birds live and what they eat. Most birds have skeletons that are strong but hollow, which makes them light enough to fly, and, like fish, birds have air sacs that both provide oxygen and make the bird lighter. Most birds have contour feathers on their body surface that are often either camouflage, helping the bird blend into its surroundings, or are very colorful, helping to attract the opposite sex. Feathers help birds steer when flying, and tiny, fluffy feathers known as "down" also trap air next to the bodies to keep birds warm.

Mammals are endotherms that breath with lungs, have hair (which warms and protects them), usually give birth to live young, feed their young with mother's milk, and are cared for by their parents. Compared to other animals, a mammal has a complex nervous system, with a well-developed brain, spinal cord, and nerves. Mammals reproduce with internal fertilization and two sexes, and they take their name from the mammary glands of females, which swell and fill with milk that feeds the young when they are born. Feeding usually goes on for some time, since, typically, young mammals need a long period of care and feeding, although different species develop at different rates.

There are three major categories of mammals, designated by how their embryos develop. Unlike other mammals, the first group, monotremes, lays eggs and incubates them for about ten days, then nurses their young on milk that seeps out of the skin around their mammary glands. There are only three kinds of monotremes in existence, the duck-billed platypus and two kinds of spiny anteaters. The second group, marsupials, give birth to offspring that are not fully developed and that live in a pouch on the mother, feeding off a nipple there, until they are grown. This group includes kangaroos and opossums.

The third group, known as placental mammals, includes most mammals, and refers to the embryo's development in the uterus of the female for a period as short as a few days and as long as two years, depending upon the kind of animal. During this time, known as the gestation period, the embryo lives in the placental sac to which it is attached by the umbilical cord, which brings the embryo food and oxygen and removes waste.

Mammals differ widely. Some, called herbivores, only eat plants, while others, called carnivores, eat meat, and a third group, omnivores, eat both. All mammals have specialized teeth, depending upon what they use their teeth for in the way of eating, cutting, or tearing. Additionally, mammals can live in very different ways—they can be burrowers in the ground or tree-climbers, they can live in the ocean (like whales and dolphins), and some, like bats, can even fly. Some mammals are very slow, while others can run very fast. Specialized feet, hooves, and even hands (as with raccoons or monkeys) abound among mammals.

Body features that an animal inherits are called "traits." Similarly, an "adaptation" is a body part or behavior that helps an animal meet its needs in its environment. For example, beaks, teeth, feet, covering, camouflage, or mimicry. Arctic hares, for example, have fur that turns white in the winter, so it won't show against the snow, and light brown in summer, so it will blend in with vegetation.

All animals also exhibit innate (inherited) behavior, often reflex (automatic) actions, such as running from fire. Instinctive behaviors may be more complex and take longer, such as a retrieving dog fetching a ball, even with no encouragement. Animals practice instinctive behaviors when they protect themselves, defend their territories, live in social groups, communicate, hibernate (take a long, deep, winter sleep that saves energy), migrate, or reproduce.

Learned behavior, like hunting or communicating, is more complex and includes several different factors. Imprinting occurs when an animal attaches itself to another organism, typically the parent, shortly after birth. Motivation, often hunger, causes an animal to act in a certain way, and animals learn new skills through motivation, often by trial and error, until they get the skill right. New behaviors can be learned by conditioning, in which a response to a stimulus is learned. The most famous conditioning experiment is that conducted by the Russian scientist Ivan Pavlov, in which he taught dogs to expect food when he rang a bell, then found he could make them salivate by ringing the bell even if no food were presented. Finally, insight is a form of reasoning in which animals apply past experiences to solve new problems, as with laboratory rats that have learned to keep trying dead ends in mazes, because in the past they have ultimately gotten to their goals.

CELLS

The cell theory is one of the major theories in science. It states that all organisms are made up of one or more cells, that cells are the basic units of all organisms, and that all cells come from cells that already exist. The invention of microscopes, starting in the late 1500s and becoming increasingly sophisticated, allowed scientists to see more and more detail of various organisms, and to learn new information about cells.

The cell is the basic structure of all living things, plant and animal. In an organism with many cells, the size and shape of the cells depend upon their different functions. Most materials move in and out of cells by diffusion—a gradual process of filtering through the cell membranes and spreading out. Since no energy is involved in the movement, it is called "passive transport," and the movement of water and dissolved materials through a series of cells is known as "osmosis," which is how the cells of plants get most of their water from the soil (and grow) or give off water to the soil (and wilt). The cell can also spend energy to use a carrier to transport materials, a process called "active transport," as the materials move in and out of the cells through a channel in the cell membrane.

Every cell has a membrane with a jelly-like material called "cytoplasm" inside it, and a hereditary material that controls the life of the cell. There are cells of various sizes and shapes, but there are two basic types. Those that have no membrane around their hereditary material are called "prokaryotic cells," and exist as one-celled organisms. Prokaryotic cells have an outer protective cell wall with a cell membrane inside that forms a container for the cytoplasm, which contains the hereditary material.

By contrast, those cells with a nucleus, which is hereditary material surrounded by a membrane, are called "eukaryotic cells." Most plants and animals are made up of eukaryotic cells. The permeable "cell membrane" is the outside layer of the cell, and food and oxygen move into the cell through the membrane, just as waste products leave the cell through the membrane. Plants have a cell wall (which supports and protects the cell) made of cellulose fibers, outside the cell membrane. The cytoplasm, the jelly-like substance inside the cell membrane, is the next layer. The cytoplasm contains water, chemicals and the organelles, which are small structures surrounded by membranes.

The nucleus in a eukaryotic cell, encased in a nuclear membrane, is an organelle that manages the cell using a long, thread-like material called chromatin, which contains proteins and DNA—the chemical that is the blueprint for the cell's make-up and activities. The nucleus also contains the nucleolus at its center. Other organelles within the cytoplasm are the endospasmic reticulum around the cell, and the ribosomes, which make specific proteins. The Golgi bodies prepare proteins to be moved outside of the cell. The mitochondria break down food molecules and release energy.

Storage organelles in the cell are called vacuoles and vesicles, they store water, waste, and food. The vacuoles are larger, and in plants they make digestive chemicals and may take up most of the room in the cell. Animal cells make digestive chemicals through lysosomes, which break down food, wastes, and worn out cell parts.

In one-celled organisms, the one cell performs all necessary functions, but cells in many-celled organisms perform different jobs, interacting to help the organisms stay alive. In animals, there may be bone cells, for example, which together form tissue, which is organized into organs that make up systems such as the skeletal, digestive, or cardiovascular systems. Ultimately, all the cells and systems work together to keep the organism alive.

Bacteria are prokaryotes—their cells have no nucleus and their organelles are not surrounded by membranes—and they are also much smaller than eukaryotic cells. The nuclear material of a bacteria cell is made up of circular chromosomes. Bacteria have cell walls, cell membranes, and ribosomes. There are three different bacteria shapes, sphere-shaped cocci, rod-shaped bacilli, and spiral-shaped spirilla. The cells of most bacteria contain cytoplasm surrounded by a cell membrane and wall, and the chromosomes are found in the cytoplasm.

REPRODUCTION

Living organisms are constantly changing as cells grow, divide, and die. Cells divide in two steps, first the nucleus and then the cytoplasm. Mitosis is the process by which the nucleus divides to form two new nuclei, each identical to the original. When the cytoplasm also separates, two new cells are formed and begin to grow. The various stages of life are called the "life cycle." Some organisms, like spiders, produce babies that look the same as the adults, only smaller, a phenomenon known as "direct development," while other organisms produce young that somewhat resemble the adults. The young of some other organisms have a complete metamorphosis, like butterflies or some insects, with four stages of development (egg, larva, pupa, adult) and very different types of bodies depending on age, or have an incomplete metamorphosis, with three stages of development (egg, nymph, and adult).

Different organisms have different ways of reproducing. There are two types of reproduction, asexual and sexual. Asexual reproduction produces a new organism with the identical hereditary material of the parent organism. Types of asexual reproduction include fission (the organism divides into two), budding (a new organism grows from the body of a single parent), and regeneration (a whole organism grows from a piece of an organism). Bacteria, for example, reproduce by fission, a type of "asexual" reproduction (meaning two sexes are not required, a bit like cloning), producing cells with genetic material identical to that of the parent cell, although some bacteria do exchange genetic material.

In plants, asexual reproduction is called vegetative propagation, and includes spider plants, strawberry plants, grass that grows new runners that turn into roots, or tubers (like potatoes) that have buds or eyes that make a new plant. Some plants, like ferns, grow from single cell spores, some form bulbs that can be separated, and some grow from stems put in water or from a cutting, such as the top of a pineapple plant. Grafting is growing a new branch or tree on the stem of the old one, often done with fruit. Tissue culture is a way to chemically encourage cells to divide and reproduce. Any time a new plant grows from part of the old, it will have the exact same genes as the parents and fewer variations and adaptabilities than one that combines the genes of two plants.

Sexual reproduction, for both plants and animals, involves an egg and a sperm, usually from two different organisms, joining together in an act called fertilization to form a new, third organism, called a "zygote." The sperm is produced in the reproductive organs of the male and the egg in the reproductive organs of the female. In recent years, scientists have managed to clone some animals (starting with the Scottish sheep "Dolly") by getting an egg to divide and form an embryo, creating a new animal with the exact hereditary make-up of its one parent. As cloning becomes more technologically successful, there is speculation that it may be used to help eliminate disease by making genetic changes in embryos.

DNA is the shorthand for deoxyribonucleic acid—an organism's chemical information code that determines the shape and function of a cell and that controls all the activities of the cell. DNA makes up chromosomes, which are inside the nucleus and tell a cell when to divide. DNA was discovered in the 1950s, when Rosalind Franklin found that the DNA molecule formed two strands in a double spiral form, and James Watson and Francis Crick made the first model of a DNA molecule. DNA contains all the essential information for various traits such as height and eye and skin color, is expressed through proteins made of amino acids, and it copies itself for reproduction. Protein is made on ribosomes in cytoplasm, and the code from the nucleus is carried to the ribosomes by three kinds of ribonucleic acid, known as RNA, made from DNA. Sometimes an error is made in the reproduction of a gene, which means a trait of the organism changes. This is called a mutation, and could be good or bad, or could have little effect on the organism.

Inherited traits are characteristics of organisms passed to their offspring, such as hair color, or eye color, or inherited behaviors, such as dogs being able to swim. The Austrian monk Gregor Mendel worked with pea plants in the 1860s and observed that some produced green peas and others yellow peas, and that when he crossbred a tall with a short, all the first generation offspring were tall. When Mendel bred two talls, three were tall and one was short in the second generation. He said that for every trait, an offspring inherits one factor from each parent, and the way the factors combine determines which trait appears in the offspring. Mendel hypothesized that the tall plants must have had a hidden factor for shortness. Tallness was a dominant trait and shortness a recessive trait, so he said recessive traits could be seen only if both parents pass the factor for it to the offspring. What Mendel called factors are now called genes, and they contain the DNA codes for the traits an organism inherits.

In angiosperms, most reproductive parts are in flowers and often are contained in the same flower. Male parts are called stamens and produce pollen at their tops, called "anthers." Female parts are called "pistils" and produce eggs. Before blooming, the flower petals and reproduction parts are tightly closed in a bud that is covered by "sepals." When the flower blooms, the pistil is usually in the center of the flower and is made up of a long, narrow tube called the "style." The top of the pistil is the "stigma," which is often sticky to hold pollen. Pollen carried by wind or insects from stamens of one flower to pistils of another is called "cross-pollination," and it allows genetic traits to spread and help the plants survive, although some flowers can pollinate themselves. Bright flowers, sweet liquid (known as "nectar"), pleasant smells, and food all attract insects and animals to flowers. The animals feed on plants, and in doing so, they move from plant to plant, inadvertently spreading pollen, which helps flowers form seeds.

When a pollen grain lands on the stigma, a tube begins to grow from a cell in the pollen down a trough in the style to an opening in the ovary, which is at the bottom of the pistil and has eggs in sections called "ovules." The sperm cells move down the pollen tube and into an ovule, and fertilization occurs when a sperm cell joins with an egg to form a zygote. Seeds and their protective fruit develop in the pistil. Animals also spread seeds by eating them, then eliminating them elsewhere. Wind and water also spread seeds.

The main parts of a seed are the seed coat, the seedling, and the stored food. Inside the seed is an embryo surrounded by food stored in cotyledons, or embryo leaves. A plant with one cotyledon is called a monocotyledon (monocot) and a plant with two is called a dicotyledon (dicot). The seed germinates, or sprouts, by taking in water which makes the seed coat swell and split. Then the embryo grows and develops roots and a stem, and the seedling uses the stored food in the cotyledons until the real leaves grow and make food, and the cotyledons drop off.

THE HUMAN BODY

The human body is made of cells that form tissue in organs, and it has various body parts to do specific jobs. The body is covered by skin, which has about 150,000 cells in every square centimeter. The top layer cells (the epidermis) are always dying, but skin cells replace themselves very quickly, by dividing in two—the top layer of skin is replaced about twice a day. Under the skin are bones, muscles, and various organs. A group of organs that have a particular function is called a system. The human body is very complex and is made up of several systems, including the skeletal system, the endocrine system, the muscular system, the respiratory system, the circulatory system, the digestive system, the excretory system, and the nervous system.

The skeletal system is the framework for the body. The skeleton is made up of bones that fit together to make a skeleton and to support the body and give it shape and protection. The rib cage, for example, protects the heart, and the skull protects the brain. Bones are living organs, each made up of an outer protective membrane, a layer of hard material, and a softer center containing bone marrow that produces both red and white blood cells.

There are many kinds and shapes of bones, and the points where they meet and are attached to each other and to muscles are called "joints." Hinge joints allow back and forth motion, ball and socket joints allow circular motion, and there are some bones, like the skull, with no motion. Muscles are attached to bones on each side of joints by tendons, and bones are attached to each other by ligaments—connective tissue that holds the skeleton together. There are 206 bones in the human skeleton. Each hand has 27 bones (14 bones in the fingers, 8 in the wrist, and 5 in the palm), each foot has 26 bones, and the skull has 23 bones. The ears and tip of the nose are made of cartilage, a bone-like, flexible, connective tissue that also coats the end of bones where they meet at a joint to allow smooth movement between them.

The endocrine system controls the glands in the body, through chemicals known as hormones. The major endocrine glands are the pituitary (which controls the overall endocrine glands, growth, and milk production), the thyroid (which controls carbohydrate use), the parathyroids (which control calcium), the adrenal (which control blood sugar, salt and water, and metabolism), the pancreas (which controls blood sugar and neutralizes stomach acids), the ovaries (which control sex organ development and egg production in females), and the testes (which control sex organ development and sperm production in males).

The muscular system has muscles that move bones and pump blood. Exercise and healthy food strengthen muscles. There are three main types of muscles. Skeletal muscles (also called voluntary muscles) can only pull, and they are striated light and dark, with some fibers a foot long. Cardiac muscles are unconscious, and they squeeze and relax the heart. Smooth muscles, like cardiac muscles, are also involuntary, and they squeeze and relax but they have short fibers and no stripes. Together, voluntary, smooth, and cardiac muscles make up the walls of the heart, pump blood, and set heartbeat rate.

The respiratory system is made up of body parts that take in air and oxygen and that give off air and carbon dioxide (mixed with a little oxygen, which is why artificial respiration is sometimes successful. Air ideally enters the body through the nose, where it is moistened and warmed, and where mucus and cilia (tiny hairs) trap dust as the air moves to the pharynx (it can also enter through the mouth, going straight to the pharynx at the back of the mouth). The respiratory system is very complex, and the main organs of the respiratory system are the lungs, with which the body takes in oxygen and gives off carbon dioxide. Humans breath by moving air in and out of their lungs. The fresh air contains oxygen, which goes into the circulatory system and is passed to the lungs, helping to release energy from glucose, a process called "respiration." Carbon dioxide, a waste product of respiration, is carried back to the lungs, exhaled with the used air, and ultimately used by plants to create oxygen again. Lungs not only enable people to breathe, but also help regulate the heart rate—how fast or slow the heart beats. Below the lungs is the diaphragm—a muscle that contracts and relaxes to help let air in and out of the body.

When the air first moves down the esophagus—a tube into the lungs—the lungs fill with air and get larger (this also helps a person to float). The heart helps by pumping blood with oxygen around the body, a process known as blood circulation. The pharynx is a tube for both air and food, with a cover called the epiglottis, which lets air enter the larynx and blocks food or liquid, sending it on to the esophagus. If the epiglottis does not close quickly enough to block material from entering the trachea, the person chokes and may die. The Heimlich maneuver can save lives by someone embracing the victim from behind and forcing the diaphragm below the lungs up with a sudden, sharp movement, to bring air pressure from below and dislodge the object.

Below the larynx is the trachea, lined with mucous and cilia to trap dust and bacteria. The trachea branches into two parts, called the bronchi, one for each lung, both lined with small hairs and coated with mucus that traps germs and dirt as the small hairs sweep the mucus up and out, keeping the lungs clear. Within each lung, the bronchi branch into multiple tubes called the bronchiole, which have clusters of alveoli, little thin-walled air sacs, at the end of them, surrounded by tiny blood vessels called "capillaries," where the oxygen and carbon dioxide are passed back and forth, as the exchange of air takes place. The respiratory system can be damaged by smoking, polluted air, and disease. Bronchitis, emphysema, asthma, and lung cancer are all diseases of the respiratory system.

The capillaries, mentioned above, are part of the circulatory system. The circulatory system also includes the heart and various blood vessels—the tubes blood flows through. The heart is a muscle that pumps out blood through the arteries, which become capillaries that carry blood with oxygen to every cell, then capillaries become pulmonary veins—the large blood vessels that return the blood to the heart.

Red blood cells carry oxygen from the lungs to the rest of the body and carry carbon dioxide from the rest of the body back to the lungs, so it can be breathed out. Blood also contains white blood cells, which attack and kill invading germs or infected cells, and platelets, which clot blood by clumping together—the clump traps red blood cells to form a scab and seal any cuts.

The heart and lungs work together to bring in oxygen and take out carbon dioxide. The heart has four chambers, and each acts as a pump with a valve. Blood flows in one direction—from the lungs to the main part of heart and to the rest of the body, then returns from the rest of the body to the lungs.

The digestive system begins with a person eating, with teeth and saliva in the mouth helping to mechanically and chemically break down the food, which goes down the esophagus to the stomach. In the stomach, muscles and digestive juices (known as "gastric juices") containing acid and chemicals break the proteins and food down further until they are mostly liquid. The liver produces bile, which is stored in the gallbladder until needed, as it breaks down fats into small particles that can be more easily digested. The partially digested food then moves from the stomach into the small intestine, where digestion is completed as the nutrients enter the blood, and the capillaries carry the nutrients to cells in all parts of the body. Villi—projections sticking out of the walls of the small intestine—diffuse the leftover wastes to the large intestine, known as the "bowel," which removes the water, then eliminates them.

Another system in the body is the excretory system, which eliminates waste products. It includes the digestive system (which gives off solids, as explained above), the urinary system (which gives off salts and excess water), and the previously-mentioned circulatory and respiratory systems (which also give off gas and salts from sweat). Together these systems make up the excretory system. The two bean-shaped kidneys, located at the back of the waist, are the major organs of the urinary system. Each kidney is made up of nephrons, tiny filtering units that filter the blood, which collects waste (urine) from cells. The urine goes through tubes called "ureters" to the bladder, which holds the urine until it leaves the body through the tube called the "urethra."

Water also leaves the body through perspiration, exhalation, and excreted solids. Fluid levels in the body are regulated, as is blood pressure, from a part of the brain called the hypothalamus, which controls the body's homeostasis, or steady internal body conditions. The brain sends thirst signals when the body needs more water. When the urinary system is not working properly, waste products can collect as water builds up, poisoning the body and causing swelling of feet and ankles, which makes the heart work harder to move blood to the lungs. If the kidneys are damaged, the person may need to have dialysis, which is the filtering of the blood by machine to remove waste.

The nervous system controls all parts of the body, and the brain is the center of the nervous system. The nervous system is made up of nerve cells, and it helps the body respond to stimuli—changes in environment, such as noises, temperature, events, or even drugs, which affect the inner environment of the body. Each nerve cell, called a neuron, contains a cell body, branches called dendrites (which receive messages, called "impulses," and send them to the cell body), and axons (which carry messages, also called impulses, away from the cell body). The three types of neurons are sensory neurons (which receive information and send impulses to the brain or spinal cord), interneurons (which send the impulses from the sensory neurons to the motor neurons), and motor neurons (which conduct impulses from the brain or spinal cord to muscles and glands throughout the body). Since the neurons do not touch each other, the spaces between them, called synapses, are bridged by a chemical that moves across the synapse to the next neuron.

The nervous system is divided into two main parts. The first is the central nervous system, known as the CNS, which includes the brain and the spinal cord. In the CNS, the brain is protected by the bones of the skull, and the spinal cord is protected by the bones of the vertebrae. Membranes and cerebrospinal fluid also protect the CNS. Within the CNS, the brain is made up of billions of neurons and is divided into three parts. The cerebrum, which is the largest part, stores memory, controls the voluntary muscles, and interprets impulses from the senses. The cerebrum is made up of two hemispheres and an outer layer, called the "cortex," which is shaped into ridges and grooves. Like the cerebrum, the cerebellum also controls voluntary muscle movements, as well as maintaining balance and muscle tone.

The brain stem connects the brain to the spinal cord—a tube of nerves that runs through the backbone. The brain stem regulates heartbeat, breathing, and blood pressure by controlling involuntary muscle movements. The brain stem is made up of the midbrain, the pons, and the medulla. The spinal cord extends from the brain stem and is made up of bundles of neurons that carry impulses from all parts of the body to the brain and back (the brain gets a lot of information from the organs).

The second major part of the nervous system is called the peripheral nervous system, or PNS. It includes the cranial and spinal nerves, as well as all the nerves outside the CNS. The PNS also has two parts. First, the somatic system includes the cranial and spinal nerves that lead from the CNS to the skeletal muscles. The second part, the autonomic system, controls heartbeat, breathing, digestion, and gland functions.

The five senses are seeing, hearing, smelling, tasting, and touching. The sense of sight is perhaps the one that most people would least like to do without. Sight is based on reaction to light, which is bent by the cornea and lens as light enters the eye. The lens directs the rays of light to the retina, a tissue at the back of the eye, which contains two types of cells, rods and cones. Cones respond to bright light and color, and rods to dim light, shape, and movement. Light energy stimulates rods and cones to send impulses to the optic nerve, which carries them to the brain to interpret the image. Depending upon whether lenses are convex (bulging out) or concave (bending in), the light may be bent in different rays. Manmade lenses, glasses, can be used to correct flaws in the eye's natural shape.

Hearing is based on sound energy that creates sound waves which travel through the outer ear to vibrate on the eardrum in the middle ear. These waves move through three little bones called the hammer, the anvil, and the stirrup, which rests against the inner ear, vibrating fluid in the snail-shaped cochlea in the inner ear. The vibrations stimulate nerve cells in the ear and send impulses to the brain, which interprets the sounds. The inner ear also controls balance, as structures and fluid there adjust continuously to the position of the head, sending impulses to the brain to make any necessary adjustments to maintain balance.

The sense of smell is based on olfactory nerves in the nasal passages picking up gas molecules, from food, in the air. The gas molecules dissolve in the nasal mucous, and the cells become stimulated, sending impulses to the brain, which interprets the stimulus as smell. If the nose is blocked up, food seems tasteless because the gaseous food molecules cannot contact the membranes in the nose—showing that the sense of smell is intertwined with the sense of taste.

The sense of taste is based on taste buds on the tongue which respond to chemical stimuli. At the prospect of food, the mouth starts to "water" with saliva, which helps dissolve the food when it arrives. The four basic taste sensations, combined in endless combinations, are sweet, salty, sour, and bitter.

The sense of touch is based on many different types of sensory receptors throughout the skin and in the internal organs. These sensory receptors pick up changes in touch, pressure, and temperature and transmit the impulses to the brain, so the body responds to protect itself or maintain homeostasis (internal stability). Some parts of the body, like the lips and fingers, have more sensors, making them more sensitive to various stimuli.

In order to keep the human body healthy, it is important to take in the right amounts of protein, roughage, glucose, and vitamins. The food pyramid put out by the United States government suggests 6–11 daily servings of carbohydrates (bread, cereal, rice), 2–4 daily servings of vegetables and fruit, 2–3 daily servings of dairy products and meat or other protein, and very light consumption of fats and sweets. The food pyramid replaced the balanced food groups chart that had been used for years, as the chart suggested higher consumption of dairy and meats. There is still controversy about whether the recommendations on the food pyramid of carbohydrates and dairy are too high. There does, however, seem to be general agreement that too many fats and sweets are not good for people, and, in fact, seem to be contributing, along with carbohydrates and large portion size, to the increasing proportion of the population that is overweight.

Not everyone who eats right is healthy, however, and the causes of disease have baffled doctors and scientists throughout human history. Even today some diseases, like Parkinson's disease or multiple sclerosis, appear mysteriously, but, through much painstaking scientific research, the causes of many diseases are known. Diseases are caused by viruses, protozoans, and/or harmful bacteria known as pathogens. Louis Pasteur, a French scientist of the 1800s, theorized that bacteria could cause disease, and he discovered that heating bacteria could kill it. This process—known as "pasteurization"—is still used in processing drinks, especially milk and canned food. A German doctor, Robert Koch, developed a way to grow one type of bacterium at a time and, through careful control and experimentation, to figure out which one caused which disease. The English doctor, Joseph Lister, suggested that handwashing and general cleanliness would kill bacteria, especially in medical settings, and he invented disinfectant to kill bacteria on surgical instruments and other surfaces. Later scientists followed up with antiseptics, which kill bacteria on skin. It was, however, some time before scientists realized that viruses, fungi, and protists could also cause disease.

A virus is nonliving and is made up of a core of hereditary material surrounded by protein. It does not grow or eat; it does reproduce, but only inside a living cell, called a "host cell." Viruses are classified by the kind of organism they infect, by their shape, by the kind of hereditary material they have, or by their method of reproduction, and are often named for the diseases they cause. When a virus enters a cell, the virus can be active, causing the host cell to make new viruses, which destroy the host cell, or the virus may be latent. The hereditary material of a latent virus becomes part of the cell's hereditary material, and it can become active any time, sometimes taking years to show up.

There are no cures for viral diseases, but some can be prevented by vaccinations—shots of damaged virus particles that no longer can cause infection but can encourage the body to create resistance to an undamaged virus of the same type. There are vaccinations for measles, chicken pox, polio, rabies, smallpox, mumps, and other viruses. Since the introduction of vaccinations, far fewer people have been infected with, or died of, those diseases. Oddly enough, viruses can sometimes be helpful in substituting normal hereditary material for a cell's defective hereditary material, a experimental process known as "gene therapy" that holds the potential to help eliminate some hereditary diseases.

Harmful bacteria are called "pathogens," and they produce diseases such as strep throat and anthrax. They are treated with antibiotics—substances produced by one organism that inhibit or kill other organisms—or are prevented, like viral diseases, with vaccinations. Some bacterial pathogens produce poisons called toxins. Botulism, a deadly type of food poisoning, is an example of an illness caused by a toxin. These bacteria often have thick walls called "endospores" around them, and they are often anaerobes, that can survive without oxygen in harsh conditions, so they are difficult to kill.

Diseases, such as flu, food poisoning, or AIDS, that are spread by infected organisms or the environment, are called "communicable diseases." These diseases are often spread through water, air (sneezing), food, contact (including sexual contact), or "biological vectors," carriers such as mosquitoes, rats, or flies. Chemicals also can cause disease, and substances known as allergens can trigger allergic responses, causing shock and even death.

However, not every exposure to pathogens causes disease to develop, since the body has ways of protecting itself. The immune system is a complex group of defenses made up of cells, tissues, organs, and body systems. Skin prevents pathogens from entering the body, the respiratory system traps them, the digestive system tries to destroy them, hydrochloric acid in the stomach kills them, white blood cells digest them, and fever slows their growth. All of those defenses help defeat disease by battling the antigens, proteins, and chemicals that ride on the surface of pathogens.

Active immunity is created when the body forms specific defenses, called "antibodies," against specific antigens. When there are enough antibodies, the antigen is defeated and the person gets better. Passive immunity is created when the antibodies, which have been produced elsewhere, are introduced into the body (as with infant vaccination). Once the specific antibodies are present, some diseases never occur.

Other diseases, such as diabetes and cancer, are called "noncommunicable diseases" because they do not spread from one person to another. Either kind of disease, communicable or noncommunicable, can be "chronic," meaning "ongoing." Some chronic diseases can be cured and others cannot. Sometimes a body with a faulty immune system turns against itself, making antibodies against its own normal proteins, with the result that the antibodies cause problems, as in rheumatoid arthritis.

READINGS FOR STUDENTS

Arnold, C. (1997). *Bat*. New York: Morrow.

Arnold, C. (1997). *Fox*. New York: Morrow.

Arnold, C. (1998). *Hawk Highway in the Sky: Watching Raptor Migration*. San Diego: Gulliver.

Arnold, C. (1997). *Rhino*. New York: Morrow.

Arnosky, J. (1997). *All about Deer*. New York: Scholastic.

Arnosky, J. (1997). *All about Owls*. New York: Scholastic Hardcover.

Arnosky, J. (1997). *I See Animals Hiding*. New York: Scholastic Hardcover.

Arnosky, J. (1998). *Watching Water Birds*. Washington D.C.: National Geographic.

Awan, S. (1998). *The Burrow Book: Tunnel into a World of Wildlife*. New York: DK Publishing.

Barfuss, M. (1999). *My Cheetah Family* (Carolrhoda Photo Books Series). Minneapolis: Carolrhoda/Lerner.

Barrett, P. (2001). *National Geographic Dinosaurs*. Washington D.C.: National Geographic.

Bernard, R. (2001). *Insects*. Washington D.C.: National Geographic Society.

Booth, J. (1997). *You Animal!* San Diego: Gulliver Green/Harcourt Brace.

Brandenburg, J. (1997). *An American Safari: Adventures on the North American Prairie*. New York: Walker.

Brenner, B. (1998). *Thinking about Ants*. Boulder: Mondo.

Brown, R. (2001). *Ten Seeds*. New York: Alfred A. Knopf/Random House Children's Books.

Browne, P. (1997). *African Animals ABC*. San Francisco: Sierra Club.

Burnie, D. (1997). *The Concise Encyclopedia of the Human Body*. New York: DK Publishing.

Butterfield, M. (1997). *Richard Orr's Nature Cross-sections*. New York: DK Publishing.

Cassie, B. (1999). *National Audubon Society First Field Guide: Trees*. New York: Scholastic Reference.

Castner, J. (2001). *Rainforest Researchers.* Salt Lake City: Benchmark Books/Marshall Cavendish.

Cerullo, M. (2001). *Sea Soup: Zooplankton.* Gardiner: Tilbury House.

Chorlton, W. (2001). *Wooly Mammoth: Life, Death, and Rediscovery.* New York: Scholastic, Inc.

Clark, M. (1997). *The Threatened Florida Black Bear.* New York: Cobblehill.

Collard, S. (2000). *The Forest in the Clouds.* Watertown: Charlesbridge.

Cowley, J. (1999). *Red-eyed Tree Frog.* New York: Scholastic Press.

Curtis, P. (1998). *Animals You Never Even Heard Of.* San Francisco: Sierra Club.

Dingus, L. and Norell, M. (1997). *Searching for Velociraptor.* New York: HarperCollins.

Dudley, K. (1998). *Wolves.* Austin: Raintree/Steck-Vaughn.

Dudzinski, K. (2000). *Meeting Dolphins: My Adventures in the Sea.* Washington D.C.: National Geographic.

Dunphy, M. (1999). *Here Is the African Savanna.* New York: Hyperion.

Earle, S. (1999). *Hello, Fish! Visiting the Coral Reef.* Washington D.C.: National Geographic.

Earle, S. (2000). *Sea Critters.* Washington D.C.: National Geographic Society.

Fraser, M. (1999). *Where Are the Night Animals?* (Let's-Read-and-Find-Out Science Series). New York: HarperCollins.

Fredricks, A. (2000). *Slugs.* Minneapolis: Lerner Publications.

Froman, N. (2001). *What's that Bug?* Boston: Little, Brown.

Gallimard. (1997). *Trees and Forests.* New York: Scholastic Inc/Gallimard Jeunesse.

Garland, S. (1997). *The Summer Sands.* San Diego: Gulliver.

George, H. (1999). *Around the World: Who's Been Here?* New York: Green-willow/HarperCollins.

George, T. (2000). *Jellies: The Life of Jellyfish.* Brookfield, CT: Millbrook Press.

Gibbons, G. (1998). *Gulls...Gulls...Gulls...* New York: Holiday House.

Gibbons, G. (1999). *The Pumpkin Book.* New York: Holiday House.

Gibbons, G. (1997). *Sea Turtles.* New York: Holiday House.

Gillette, J. (1998). *Dinosaur Ghosts: The Mystery of Coelophysis.* New York: Dial BFYR.

Goodall, J. (2001). *The Chimpanzees I Love: Saving Their World and Ours.* New York: Scholastic.

Goodman, S. (2001). *Claws, Coats, and Camouflage: The Ways Animals Fit into Their World.* Brookfield, CT: Millbrook Press.

Goodman, S. (2001). *Seeds, Stems, and Stamens: The Ways Plants Fit into Their World.* Brookfield, CT: Millbrook Press.

Grace, E. (1997). *Apes.* San Francisco: Sierra Club.

Gruper, J. (1998). *Destination: Rain Forest.* Washington D.C.: National Geographic.

Hariton, A. (1997). *Butterfly Story.* New York: Dutton.

Heiligman, D. (1997). *From Caterpillar to Butterfly.* New York: HarperCollins.

Heinz, B. (2000). *Butternut Hollow Pond.* Brookfield, CT: Millbrook Press.

Himmelman, J. (1999). *A Pill Bug's Life* (Nature Up Close Series). New York: Children's Press/Grolier.

Hiscock, B. (2001). *Coyote and Badger: Desert Hunters of the Southwest.* Honesdale: Boyds Mills Press.

Horenstein, H. (1999). *A Is for...? A Photographer's Alphabet of Animals.* San Diego: Gulliver/Harcourt Brace.

Horowitz, R. (2000). *Crab Moon.* Cambridge: Candlewick Press.

Hunt, J. (1997). *Insects.* Parsippany, NJ: Silver Burdett.

Jackson, D. (2001). *Twin Tales: The Magic and Mystery of Multiple Birth.* Boston: Megan TinleyBooks: Little, Brown.

Janulewicz, M. (1998). *Yikes! Your Body up Close!* New York: Simon and Schuster.

Jarrow, G. and Sherman, P. (1997). *The Naked Mole-ray Mystery: Scientific Sleuths at Work.* Minneapolis: Lerner.

Jenkins, M. (1999). *The Emperor's Egg.* Cambridge: Candlewick.

Jenkins, S. (1997). *Biggest, Strongest, Fastest.* Boston: Ticknor/Houghton Mifflin.

Jenkins, S. (1998). *What Do You Do When Something Wants to Eat You?* Boston: Houghton Mifflin.

Johnson, J. (2000). *National Geographic Animal Encyclopedia.* Washington D.C.: National Geographic Society.

Johnson, J. (1997). *Simon and Schuster Children's Guide to Birds.* New York: Simon and Schuster.

Johnson, J. (1998). *Simon and Schuster Children's Guide to Insects and Spiders.* New York: Simon and Schuster.

Johnson, S. (1997). *Raptor Rescue: An Eagle Flies Free.* New York: Dutton.

Jordan, T. (1997). *Angel Falls: A South American Journey.* New York: Kingfisher.

Judson, K. (2001). *Medical Ethics: Life and Death Issues.* Berkley Heights: Enslow Publishing.

Kaner, E. (1999). *Animal Defenses: How Animals Protect Themselves.* Toronto, Ontario: Kids Can Press.

Kerley, B. (2001). *The Dinosaurs of Waterhouse Hawkins.* New York: Scholastic Press.

Kovacs, D. and Madin, K. (1997). *Beneath Blue Waters: Meetings with Remarkable Deep-sea Creatures.* New York: Viking.

Kress, S. (1998). *Project Puffin: How We Brought Puffins Back to Egg Rock.* Gardiner, MA: Tilbury.

Kroll, V. (1997). *Sweet Magnolia.* Watertown, MA: Charlesbridge.

Kudlinski, K. (1999). *Dandelions* (Early Bird Nature Book Series). Minneapolis: Lerner.

Lang, S. (1997). *Nature in Your Backyard: Simple Activities for Children.* Brookfield, CT: Millbrook Press.

Lasky, K. (2001). *Interrupted Journey: Saving Endangered Sea Turtles.* Cambridge: Candlewick Press.

Lasky, K. (1998). *The Most Beautiful Roof in the World: Exploring the Rainforest Canopy.* San Diego: Gulliver.

Lauber, P. (1997). *How Dinosaurs Came to Be.* New York: Simon and Schuster.

Lauber, P. (1997). *Who Eats What? Food Chains and Food Webs.* New York: HarperCollins.

Laukel, H. (1997). *The Desert Fox Family Book.* San Francisco: North-South.

Lessem, D. (1997). *Dinosaur Worlds: New Dinosaurs, New Discoveries.* Honesdale, PA: Boyds Mills Press.

Levenson, G. (1999). *Pumpkin Circle.* Berkley Heights: Tricycle/Ten Speed.

Lewin, T. and Lewin, B. (2000). *Elephant Quest.* New York: HarperCollins.

Lewin, T. and Lewin, B. (1999). *Gorilla Walk.* New York: Lothrop/HarperCollins.

Locker, T. and Christiansen, C. (1997). *Sky Tree: Seeing Through Art.* New York: HarperCollins.

MacMillan, D. (1998). *Cheetahs.* Minneapolis: Carolrhoda.

Markle, S. (1999). *Outside and Inside Kangaroos* (Outside and Inside Series). New York: Atheneum/Simon and Schuster.

Mattison, C. (1999). *Snake.* New York: DK Publishing.

McMillan, B. (1997). *Nights of the Pufflings.* Boston: Houghton Mifflin.

McMillan, B. (1997). *Puffins Climb, Penguins Rhyme.* San Diego: Gulliver.

McMillan, B. (1997). *Summer Ice: Life Along the Antarctic Peninsula.* Boston: Houghton Mifflin.

McMillan, B. (1998). *Wild Flamingos.* Boston: Houghton Mifflin.

Micucci, C. (1997). *The Life and Times of the Honeybee.* Boston: Ticknor/Houghton Mifflin.

Miller, D. (1997). *Flight of the Golden Plover: The Amazing Migration Between Hawaii and Alaska.* Seattle: Alaska Northwest/Graphic Arts Center.

Miller, D. (2000). *River of Life.* New York: Clarion Books.

Moss, M. (2000). *This Is the Tree.* La Jolla, CA: Kane/Miller.

Nagda, A. and Bickel, C. (2000). *Tiger Math: Learning to Graph from a Baby Tiger.* New York: Henry Holt.

Nirgiotis, N. and T. (1997). *No More Dodos: How Zoos Help Endangered Wildlife.* Minneapolis: Lerner.

Oppenheim, J. (1997). *Have You Seen Trees?* New York: Scholastic.

Orensteid, R. (2001). *New Animal Discoveries.* Brookfield, CT: Millbrook Press.

Orr, R. (1998). *The Burrow Book: Tunnel into a World of Wildlife.* New York: DK Publishing.

Pandell, K. (1997). *Animal Action ABC.* New York: Dutton.

Patent, D. (1998). *Back to the Wild.* San Diego: Gulliver.

Patent, D. (1997). *Eagles of America.* New York: Holiday.

Patent, D. (1198). *Pigeons.* New York: Clarion.

Patent, D. (1997). *Return of the Wolf.* New York: Clarion.

Patent, D. (2000). *Slinky Scaly Slithery Snakes.* New York: Walker.

Pfeffer, W. (1998). *A Log's Life.* New York: Simon and Schuster.

Pfeffer, W. (1997). *Mute Swans.* Parsippany, NJ: Silver.

Pine, J. (1997). *Trees.* New York: HarperCollins.

Pirotta, S. (1998). *Turtle Bay.* New York: Farrar.

Porte, B. (1998). *Tale of a Tadpole.* London: Orchard.

Posada, M. (2000). *Dandelions: Stars in the Grass.* Minneapolis: Carolrhoda Books/Lerner.

Pringle, L. (1998). *Elephant Woman: Cynthia Moss Explores the World of Elephants.* New York: Atheneum.

Pringle, L. (1998). *Everybody Has a Bellybutton: Your Life Before You Were Born.* Honesdale, PA: Boyds Mills Press.

Pringle, L. (1997). *Fire in the Forest: A Cycle of Growth and Renewal.* New York: Atheneum.

Quinlan, S. (1997). *The Case of the Mummified Pigs and Other Mysteries in Nature.* Honesdale, PA: Boyds Mills Press.

Reed-Jones, C. (2001). *Salmon Stream.* Nevada City: Dawn Publications.

Remond, I. (2001). *The Elephant Book: For the Elefriends Campaign.* Cambridge: Candlewick Press.

Riley, L. (1997). *Elephants Swim.* Boston: Houghton Mifflin.

Ring, E. (1997). *Lucky Mouse.* Brookfield, CT: Millbrook.

Rockwell, A. (2001). *Bugs Are Insects.* New York: HarperCollins.

Ross, M. (1998). *Bird Watching with Margaret Morse Nice.* Minneapolis: Carolrhoda.

Ross, M. (2000). *Pond Watching with Ann Morgan.* Minneapolis: Carolrhoda Books/Lerner.

Ryden, H. (2001). *Wildflowers Around the Year.* New York: Clarion Books.

Sandeman, A. (1997). *Babies.* Brookfield, CT: Copper Beach/Millbrook.

Sandeman, A. (1997). *Blood.* Brookfield, CT: Copper Beach/Millbrook.

Sandeman, A. (1997). *Bones.* Brookfield, CT: Millbrook.

Sanders, S. (1999). *Crawdad Creek.* Washington D.C.: National Geographic.

Sattler, H. (1997). *The Book of North American Owls.* New York: Clarion.

Savage, S. (1997). *Butterfly.* New York: Thomson.

Savage, S. (1997). *Eyes.* New York: Thomson.

Sayre, A. (2001). *Dig, Wait, Listen: A Desert Toad's Tale.* New York: Greenwillow Books.

Schlein, M. (1998). *What's a Penguin Doing in a Place Like This?* Brookfield, CT: Millbrook Press.

Schnur, S. (2000). *Spring Thaw.* New York: Viking.

Schories, P. (1997). *Over Under in the Garden: An Alphabet Book.* New York: Simon and Schuster.

Schuch, S. (1999). *A Symphony of Whales.* San Diego: Harcourt Brace/Harcourt Trade.

Serafini, K. (2001). *Salamander Rain: A Lake & Pond Journal.* Nevada City: Dawn Publications.

Settel, J. (1999). *Exploding Ants: Amazing Facts about How Animals Adapt.* New York: Atheneum/Simon and Schuster.

Shetterly, S. (1999). *Shelterwood.* Gardiner, ME: Tilbury House.

Sill, C. (1998). *About Mammals: A Guide for Children.* Atlanta: Peachtree.

Silver. (1997). *Woods.* New York: Scientific American.

Silver, M. (1997). *Who Lives Here?* San Francisco: Sierra Club.

Simon, S. (1998). *The Brain: Our Nervous System.* New York: Morrow Junior Books.

Simon, S. (1999). *Crocodiles & Alligators.* New York: HarperCollins.

Simon, S. (2000). *Gorillas.* New York: HarperCollins.

Simon, S. (1997). *The Heart: Our Circulatory System.* New York: Morrow.

Simon, S. (1997). *Sharks.* New York: HarperCollins.

Smith, R. (1997). *Journey of the Red Wolf.* New York: Cobblehill.

Snedden, R. (1997). *What Is a Reptile?* San Francisco: Sierra Club.

Snedden, R. (1997). *Yuck! A Big Book of Little Horrors.* New York: Simon and Schuster.

Swinburne, S. (1999). *Once a Wolf: How Wildlife Biologists Fought to Bring Back the Gray Wolf.* Boston: Houghton Mifflin.

Tagholm, S. (2000). *Animal Lives: The Rabbit.* Boston: Kingfisher.

Tagholm, S. (1999). *The Barn Owl* (Animal Lives Series). Watertown: Charlesbridge.

Tagliaferro, L. (2001). *Galapagos Islands: Nature's Delicate Balance at Risk.* Minneapolis: Lerner Publications.

Taylor, B. (1997). *Animal Homes.* New York: DK Publishing.

Thomas, P. (2000). *Marine Mammal Preservation.* Brookfield, CT: Twenty First Century Books/Millbrook Press.

Tildes, P. (1997). *Animals: Black and White.* Watertown: Charlesbridge.

Tweit, S. (1998). *City Foxes.* Denver: Denver Museum of Natural History/Alaska Northwest.

Van Zyle, J. (1999). *Baby Whale's Journey.* San Francisco: Chronicle.

Vojtech, A. (2001). *Tough Beginnings: How Baby Animals Survive.* New York: Henry Holt.

Walker, R. (2001). *DK Guide to the Human Body.* New York: DK Publishing.

Walker, R. (1997). *The Visual Dictionary of the Skeleton.* New York: DK Publishing.

Walker, S. (2001). *Fireflies.* Minneapolis: Lerner Publications.

Webb, S. (2000). *My Season with Penguins: An Antarctic Journal.* Boston: Houghton Mifflin.

Wechsler, D. and VIREO. (1999). *Bizarre Birds.* Honesdale: Boyds Mills.

Winner, C. (1997). *Coyotes.* Minneapolis: Carolrhoda.

Winner, C. (1997). *The Sunflower Family.* Minneapolis: Carolrhoda.

Witmer, L. (1997). *The Search for the Origin of Birds.* London: Watts.

Woelflein, L. (1997). *Metamorphosis: Animals that Change.* Ottawa: Lodestar.
Wright-Frierson, V. (1997). *A Desert Scrapbook: Dawn to Dusk in the Sonoran Desert.* New York: Simon and Schuster.
Yolen, J. (2001). *Welcome to the River of Grass.* New York: G. P. Putnam's Sons.
Zuchora-Walske, C. (2000). *Leaping Grasshoppers.* Minneapolis: Lerner Publications.
Zoehfeld, K. (2001). *Dinosaur Parents, Dinosaur Young: Uncovering the Mystery of Dinosaur Families.* New York: Clarion Books.

WEBSITES

Lesson Plans
www.theteacherscorner.net/science/life/index.htm

Resources
place.scholastic.com/magicschoolbus/theme/animals.htm
place.scholastic.com/magicschoolbus/theme/life.htm

Coloring Book
www.nationalgeographic.com/coloringbook/archive/

The Biology Project
www.biology.arizona.edu/default.html

Biology Online
biology-online.org/

National Association of Biology Teachers (NABT)
www/nabt/org/

Developmental Biology
www.academicpress.com/db

Society for Developmental Biology Virtual Library
sdb.bio.purdue.edu/Other/VL_DB.html

Biology for Kids
www/biology4kids.com/

CHAPTER 4

ECOLOGY AND
THE ENVIRONMENT

The ecology movement, which began attracting much attention in the 1960s, attempts to balance human needs with preserving the environment, and preserving plants and animals on the brink of extinction. The new sciences of ecology and the environment, with such advocates as Greenpeace and the Nature Conservancy, have become increasingly influential to scientists, policy makers, and the general public. Earth Day was first celebrated in 1970, but even many years earlier there had been advocates of preserving natural resources and wild spaces, as well as endangered species of both plants and animals.

In the 1800s, John Muir helped save California's redwood forests, and, with his urging, President Theodore Roosevelt set aside great tracts of national forest to be preserved in various states. In 1946, Marjorie Stoneman Douglas wrote *The River of Grass*, which dealt with the interrelationships of nature and made the case for saving the Florida Everglades. Eugene Odum supported the idea of integrated ecosystems and wrote the first ecology textbook in 1953, and in 1963, Rachel Carson warned in her book *Silent Spring* against the dangers of chemical pesticides, particularly DDT.

The environment refers to living and nonliving things in a place. Habitat is the particular place where an animal finds the food, water, and shelter it needs. Habitats vary as animals have adapted. For example, deserts have little rain, and consequently plants and animals that do not need much water. Rain forests have a lot of rain, and plant and animal life that thrives on humidity. Woodland forests have trees and many animals that make their homes in and around those trees, including animals that hibernate. The Arctic and Antarctica are cold and windy, with ice, snow, and relatively few animals. Drought, flood, lightening, fire, and human activity can all alter habitat.

ENVIRONMENTAL INTERCONNECTION

Ecology is the study of the interactions between living things and their environment, which together form an "ecosystem." An ecosystem is an environment in which the inhabitants can meet their basic needs. Living elements of an ecosystem, such as the plants or animals, are known as "biotic factors," while the nonliving elements, such as sun, water, air, soil, rock, and temperature are called the "abiotic factors." Some ecosystems have a lot of life, and some have little.

An organism is an individual, and a group of species are a "population," while a "community" is a collection of all the populations in an ecosystem. The location where a population lives is called a "habitat," which is an environment that meets the needs of the organism. Habitats may be whole ecosystems or just small parts of one. The population's role in the ecosystem is called its "niche." Green plants and some protists and monerans are producers; they make their own food. Some organisms are consumers, which eat other living things. Decomposers feed on remains or wastes of plants and animals. Together, they make up a food chain. Most ecosystems have many food chains, which overlap to form food webs.

All the ecosystems together make up the "biosphere," the portion of the earth, above and below water, that supports life. The biosphere includes the oceans, the crust, and the atmosphere, and it contains many different environments. Energy from the sun provides the energy in the biosphere. The energy is transformed by plants (producers) which are eaten by herbivores (plant-eating animals), so some of the energy is passed on to the herbivore, but most of it is given off into the atmosphere as heat. Then a carnivore (a meat-eating animal also known as a "predator") eats the herbivore, and, again, energy is transferred. Some animals are both predators and prey.

The foundation of the "energy pyramid" is the producer. The energy moves up the food chain—the order in which animals eat plants and other animals—as when a beetle eats plants, a fish eats the beetle, a bird eats the fish. By the time the top level of the "energy pyramid" is reached, the amount of energy passed on is greatly reduced. In the "energy pyramid," only ten percent of the energy that is made at any given step is passed on. For another example, plants might be eaten by grasshoppers (first level consumers), which might be eaten by snakes (second level consumers), which might be eaten by hawks (third level consumers), or a similar progression, so high level consumers usually have relatively small populations. The energy available at each link in the food chain is constantly renewed by sunlight.

Ecosystems can change due to nature (flood, fire, climate change) or by the action of people and animals, such as beavers. When their ecosystem and habitats change, plant and animal populations have to adapt, move on, or be wiped out. Island organisms are especially fragile because they may live only in one small environment which may change, so they may be wiped out entirely if they cannot adapt, where if they were spread over several areas, they could avoid extinction. Nonnative species are called "exotics," and they sometimes drive out native populations through growth or disease.

Populations change, often based on limiting factors, such as fewer plants, lack of water, or presence of predators, since competition increases with density. Carrying capacity refers to the largest number of individuals an environment can support and maintain for a long period of time. When carrying capacity is exceeded, individuals must move or die. If there were no limiting factors, the population would continue to grow, but actually the population only grows until the carrying capacity of the environment is reached.

"Symbiosis" refers to species living in close relationships and helping each other to survive, as when bees, carrying pollen from flower to flower help pollinate and create seeds, and flowers make nectar to attract bees. Animals use plants for shelter and food, building such structures as bird nests, moving seeds around, eating and making waste elsewhere, spreading seeds and creating new ecosystems as they go. When each organism provides elements the other needs, their relationship is termed "mutualism." When one partner benefits but not the other, that is called "commensilism," and when one partner benefits and the other is harmed, that is called "parasitism."

"Stability" means ecosystems have balance, but "succession" slowly changes an ecosystem into a different ecosystem. Ecological succession is the process of change from one community of organisms to another in a particular place. Climate change, fire, floods, volcanoes, and people can all cause change. Primary succession typically begins in a rocky place that does not have soil, when the first "pioneer community" of living plants moves in and, in doing so, changes the conditions by eventually decaying and forming soil. That action means the area can increasingly support other types of both plant and animal life, each of which further enriches the environment. A similar course of events, called "secondary succession," happens in a place that has soil and was previously the site of plants and animals, such as a forest after a fire. When an area has reached stability and is changing very little, which can take thousands of years, it is considered a "climax community," and may contain many different species and complex food webs.

There are six different kinds of large-scale ecosystems, known as "biomes," that vary greatly, and their make-up dictates what kinds of plants and animals they support. They are tropical rain forests, deciduous forests, grasslands, deserts, taiga, and tundra. Tropical rain forests have lush trees and greenery year round, and a wide variety of animals. Deciduous forests have trees with large, flat leaves that drop seasonally, and a wide variety of animals; grasslands have flat, open, often-fertile plains, and a wide variety of animals. Deserts have dry climates with limited plants and small animals. Taiga has mostly coniferous forests made up of evergreen trees that have needle-like leaves and animals that survive well in the cold. Tundra has seasonal low shrubs and small animals in an extremely cold winter climate.

Water habitats are usually divided into freshwater and salt water. Rivers, streams, lakes, and ponds are freshwater environments with many animals such as turtles, frogs, and fish. Freshwater ecosystems have many different kinds of depth and movement. Oceans are big, deep bodies of water that cover three-quarters of the earth and form large salt water environments with algae and many animals such as crabs, fish, lobster, and even corals—tiny living animals whose skeletons make up ocean reefs. Oceans are saltwater ecosystems that have various degrees of saltiness. Ocean zones are the intertidal zone (shallow, with the most animal life and plants), the near-shore zone (medium depth, with much animal and floating plant life) and the open-ocean zone (deep, with few plants and animals). The French scientist Jacques Cousteau did much to promote awareness of the ocean environments with his underwater explorations and studies of oceans.

Wetlands are also important environments. Wetlands can be saltwater marshes, mangrove swamps, or mud flats, and they provide habitat and act as natural filters for cleaning water. Many wetlands were filled in before people realized how important they were, and started taking steps to protect them. The Florida Everglades, for example, once covered about 4 million acres, but now, because of development and agriculture, covers less than half that.

EFFECTS OF HUMANS

Humans have a great effect on the environment, and human events can change an environment and cause extinction or the elimination of a kind of organism forever. Humans use land for growing food and for grazing livestock, they cut and/or plant trees, and they mine metals and minerals (mineral resources are valuable, but the process of mining them often harms the environment, so in recent years, laws have been passed to ensure that mining damage is repaired). Humans also pave over great swathes of land for roads and buildings, which increases water runoff, and they create landfills and hazardous wastes, including radioactive materials from nuclear power. Chemicals, logging, runoff, paving, and wastes are all products of human activity. Waste that harms land, water, or air is called pollution. Pollution can harm people, animals, and plants, as well as the physical environment. Conservation is the careful use of resources, with the hope of preserving the environment.

One form of pollution is acid rain, in which the gases released by burning oil and coal mix with water to form rain or snow, which is so acidic it can kill trees or fish when it falls on forests and lakes. It is estimated that in the United States cars produce over half of all pollution, so efforts are ongoing to urge conservation, ride sharing, and to make cars that use less gas (made from oil) and that catch some of their own pollutants before they are released into the air. For many years, there has been a movement urging more efficient public transportation and cars that use alternative fuels, such as electricity or sunlight, instead of nonrenewable resources such as fossil fuels like oil and gas. The American public, however, has resisted giving up private cars, and technical problems have kept some alternative fuels from becoming mainstream.

It is thought that as the technology improves, alternative fuels will be increasingly used because they mostly use renewable resources (that can be replaced or recycled within one hundred years, like trees) or inexhaustible resources like sun, wind, and water, which can be used again and again, as well as geothermal energy. The sun provides enormous amounts of solar energy, but the technology for capturing that energy has not been perfected. Additionally, many areas of the earth are often cloudy, and half the time is night, so solar energy has its limitations. Wind energy has some of the same advantages and disadvantages—wind is clean, free, and nonpolluting, but it does not always blow, and many parts of the world have little wind. Hydroelectric power uses the weight of water to produce energy, either naturally, as from a waterfall, or from a manmade dam. But often a dam impinges on the environment where it is built, and many areas have no excess water.

Another alternative energy source is geothermal energy, which comes from within the earth, often through geysers (when underground water turns to steam and escapes through the earth's crust), but geysers are not common enough to be used very much. A source of energy discovered in the twentieth century is nuclear energy. This form of energy is in endless supply, produced by splitting the nuclei of uranium, which causes a chain reaction and release of energy. Nuclear energy would seem to be the perfect fuel, but it has a major drawback that has prevented its spread in the United States and made it very controversial— it produces waste material that is highly radioactive for thousands of years and that can cause cancer or other harmful effects.

There are, however, many ways people can conserve and help to preserve the environment, including careful management and wise use of natural resources, including recycling (reusing a resource to make something new), which helps save energy and reduce pollution. Planting to control erosion (trees hold soil and make oxygen), reclaiming land used for mining, and even building fish ladders can all help. "Bioremediation" is using living organisms to change pollutants into harmless compounds, such as when one-celled organisms are used to eat up oil spills. "Phytoremediation" means fixing toxic areas by planting such trees as poplars, which not only are not much affected by pollution but actively process pollutants to help clean the air and soil. "Xeriscaping" is the use of water-saving methods and drought resistant plants in landscaping. Often, land cannot be restored to its original condition, but it can still be improved and made ecologically sound and useful.

The human population has increased at such a rapid rate in the last few hundred years that the growth is referred to as a "population explosion," and concern has been raised about the carrying capacity of the earth (how much life it can support). It took approximately eighty years for the human population to double from 1 to 2 billion, but only 45 years to go from 2 to 4 billion, mostly through improvements in sanitation, growing food, and wiping out disease. The current population of about 6 billion is projected to nearly double in the next hundred years if it continues to grow at the same rate. As the human population grows, the population of other living things shrinks, so at some point, it will be up to humans to decide whether to limit their numbers before too many other species become extinct or whether to wait until they are forced to do so by the carrying capacity of the earth.

Birth control is an option that is becoming increasingly important, since people have a tremendous effect on the environment by using so many resources. The average adult needs thirty pounds of air, two to three pounds of food, and four to five pounds of water daily, although the average American uses about five times more resources (including 100 gallons of water a day) than are used by the average world citizen. Food, shelter, and clothing are basic needs, but all of the wealthy, industrialized countries also use a lot of resources for things such as the following: central heating and air conditioning; hot water for daily bathing; elaborate entertainment and computer equipment; and machines like dishwashers, washing machines, and dryers that help to make work easier. However, although they use more resources, the wealthy, industrialized countries generally have the lowest birth rates and the slowest population growth, except for immigration.

There are many ways to reuse or recycle various materials, all of which help to limit waste and improve the environment, including industry cutting down on overpackaging. Many people are careful environmentalists voluntarily, and many communities encourage recycling by offering pick-up of used materials such as glass bottles, aluminum cans, and paper. One of the easiest things to recycle, in a process known as composting, is vegetation like lawn and shrub clippings, as it decomposes relatively quickly and makes rich soil. Recycling of manufactured products has more problems, since often the cost of the process leaves minuscule profits to be made off the recycled material. But as the processes get more efficient, many people hope that extensive recycling will become more common and will help the environment even more.

Air pollution is a major environmental problem, especially in many heavily populated areas. Industry generates chemical pollution, vehicles give off pollution from burning fossil fuels, and nuclear power plants create radioactive materials. Even nature contributes pollution in the form of volcanic ash and fires. Smoke, often from burning fossil fuels, and fog together create smog, a brownish or grayish haze that hangs in the air when there is little wind, or when landforms like the mountains west of Los Angeles block winds. Air pollution, especially particulates (fine, airborne solids), can cause people's eyes to water and their nose and throats and lungs to be irritated. People's brains and hearts can be affected by low oxygen levels caused by carbon monoxide.

Air pollution, mostly from cars, can also mix with rain to form acid rain, which is very destructive to forests, where it kills trees, and to freshwater lakes and ponds, where it can kill fish. Interestingly, although most attention is given to outdoor air pollution, since it is seen as a more long-term problem, according to the United Nations, three million people die annually from air pollution, most of them women and children who suffer from indoor air pollution that comes from burning wood or manure.

Freshwater and forests are becoming scarcer and sea levels rising. It is estimated that more than one billion people lack access to safe drinking water, most in Asia or Africa. Developing countries, due to regulation and activism, slightly increased forestation in the 1990s, while Africa and Asia continued to lose forests in the same years, although the rate of cutting slowed. Human activity since the Industrial Revolution and the rise of machinery has started to change the balance of the carbon dioxide–oxygen cycle, as fewer forests mean fewer plants to use carbon dioxide and make oxygen. As a result, there has been new attention to the concept of "sustainability," the idea of advancing human progress and reducing poverty without harming nature, while making sure the planet can sustain its living creatures.

As noted, there has been increased interest in preserving the environment in the second half of the twentieth century. Since then, there has been an array of laws passed to protect the environment, often over the objections of people who feel their livelihoods or industries will suffer, such as coal miners or the automobile industry, but cleaning up pollution and preserving the environment have enjoyed strong support from most people. The Environmental Protection Agency enforces laws that protect environment, and in 1972, it made use of DDT illegal and began raising endangered animals in captivity for release into the wild. The Endangered Species Act of 1973 made it illegal to contribute to the eradication of endangered species, mostly by blocking destruction of habitat, but after thirty years, just thirteen species have recovered enough to be taken off the list.

The 1987 Clean Water Act helps states build sewers and wastewater treatment plants, control runoff, and develop safe standards for streams. Since the passage of the 1990 Clean Air Act, which requires sharply reduced car exhaust and sulfur dioxide emissions, there has also been increased interest in alternative forms of nonpolluting energy such as solar, wind, and geothermal power, although the technology has yet to be perfected. In addition, the 1996 Safe Water Drinking Act improves standards for drinking water and protects the freshwater sources of drinking water.

READINGS FOR STUDENTS

Bright, M. (1987). *Pollution and Wildlife*. New York: Franklin Watts.
Bright, M. (1991). *Polluting the Oceans*. New York: Franklin Watts.

Cochran, J. (1987). *Plant Ecology.* Danbury, CT: FranklinWatts.

Coombs, K. (1996). *Flush! Treating Wastewater.* Minneapolis: Carolrhoda.

Earthbooks staff. (1991). *National Wildlife Federation's Book of Endangered Species, Wiping Out Disease, and Arthbooks.*

Gallant, R. (1991). *Earth's Vanishing Forests.* New York: Macmillan.

Hogner, D. C. (1977). *Endangered Plants.* New York: Crowell.

Kiefer, I. (1981). *Poisoned Land: The Problem of Hazardous Waste.* New York: Atheneum.

Maze, S. (2000). *I Want to Be an Environmentalist.* San Diego: Harcourt.

Miller, C. and Berry, L. (1987). *Acid Rain.* New York: Messner.

Penn, L. (1987). *Plant Ecology.* Danbury, CT: Franklin Watts.

Sabin, F. (1985). *Ecosystems and Food Chains.* Troll Associates.

Scott, M. (1997). *Ecology.* New York: Oxford.

Snodgrass, M. E. (1991). *Environmental Awareness: Water Pollution.* BSP Publications.

WEBSITES

Virtual Library of Ecology
www.conbio.net/vl/

Ecology, the Environment and Nature
www.glen-ellyn.com/environmental

Ecology "Awesome Library"
www/awesomelibrary.org/Classroom/Science/Ecology/Ecology.html

Teaching Tips
www.abc.net.au/labnotes/tips/topics/ecology.htm

Resources
place.scholastic.com/magicschoolbus/theme/ecology.htm

Environmental Education
www.missmaggie.org

Fun Social Studies
www.funsocialstudies.learninghaven.com/links/
ecology_and_the_environment.htm

Links to Ecology
www.umsl.edu/~biology/icte/links.html

Dictionary of Ecology
www.petercollin.com/Titles/English/Academic/Ecology/ecology.html

World Ecology
www.worldecology.com/

Environmental Education Programs
www.gwu.edu/~greenu/edu.html

Ecology and the Environment
www.limestone.lib.il.us/hhecology.html Endangered Rivers

Education Planet Environment
www.educationplanet.com/search/Environment/Environmental_Science/
Ecology/

Digital Field Trip to the Wetlands
www.digitalfrog.com/products.wetlands.html

Environmental Education K–12 Teachers
www.eelsinc.com/TeacherTopics.asp

Human Ecology and the Environment
www.ccd.cccoes.edu/~sci_tech/m_verde1.html

Introduced Species and the Australian Environment
bees.unsw.edu/highschool/E&ES9~5_2.html

Introduced Species and the Australian environment
www/geology.unsw.edu.au/Teachers/E&ES9~5_2.html

Kids' Ecology
www.stratford.library.on.ca/kids/subjects/science/ecology.htm

Venezuela's Eco Portal to Eco-tourism
members.tripod.com/~wildlife_vzla/articles.htm

Science for Families
scienceforfamilies.allinfo-about.com/subjects/environment.html

Georgia Youth Science and Technology Centers
www.spsu.edu/gystc/so.htm

Environmental Education
nlreep.org/environmental_ed.htm

Science/Ecology
www.sasked.gov.sk.ca/docs/midlsci/gr9vamsc.html

■ ■ ■ ■ ■

CHAPTER 5

EARTH AND OCEANS

Geology is the study of the earth. The foundation of geology was laid in the 1700s by James Hutton, who suggested the earth was constantly changing. Geology was further established in the 1800s by Charles Lyell, who wrote about the physical history and make-up of the earth. The theory of "continental drift" suggests that over 225 million years ago, all land was joined in a giant mass called "Pangea," and that it broke up into two big continents, "Gondwana" in the southern hemisphere and "Laurasia" in the northern, then into smaller land masses represented by the current continents.

The earth can be represented by both globes and maps. Globes are simply small, round three-dimensional models of the earth, so they are usually quite accurate, but because they are so small, they do not show much detail. Two-dimensional maps are much better at showing just a section of the earth, but they are inevitably distorted, because they represent a globular earth on a flat surface. Different ways of making a flat representation of the three-dimensional earth are called "projections." The most common projection is the Mercator projection, which simply represents the earth as a rectangular map, with the lines of longitude parallel to each other. The problem with this projection is that as the lines approach the poles on the earth, they get narrower and converge, but the map does not show that, so there is great distortion, with the representations of land near the poles (notably Greenland and Antarctica) being far too large. Another common but somewhat more accurate projection is the Robinson projection, which shows curved sides and lines of longitude for less distortion.

Aside from the technicalities of the representation, maps can show a variety of information. There are maps showing political divisions, landforms, and clustering of religions, populations, dietary habits, and weather. Topographic maps show the features of the earth's surface, and they can be either two-dimensional or even slightly three-dimensional (if the features actually protrude from the flat surface). All maps have scale—the relationship between the distance shown on the map and the actual distance on the earth's surface. Most maps have a legend to show what symbols mean. Remote sensing using satellites and radar have been used in recent years to make more accurate maps, and the Global Positioning System, known as GPS, makes it possible for drivers in many cars to know their exact position on earth at any given time.

The geologic time scale is a record of the earth's history based on a way of measuring the passage of time according to the changes found in fossils. Geologic time is divided into eras, based on differences in life-forms. The three eras are Paleozoic (ancient life), Mesozoic (middle life), and Cenozoic (recent life). The eras are divided into periods based on the type of life that existed during the period, and the periods are further divided into epochs, usually labelled early, middle, and late, (although the Cenozoic era, which includes the present time, has more delineated epochs because the fossil record is more complete). Reptiles became the dominant life form in the Jurassic period, evolving into dinosaurs, crocodiles, and birds.

THE MAKE-UP OF THE EARTH

The earth has a thin outer crust of rock and soil, a middle section called the "mantle," made up of thick layers of hot, hard and soft rock, and a hot inner core of iron and nickel surrounded by an outer core of liquid rock called "magma." The crust and upper mantel are in the form of slabs called "plates." An earthquake is the shaking of the ground in a discernable movement of crust and mantle caused by a sudden release of energy in the earth's crust as plates crush, scrape, or bend. There are many shifting plates along the California coastline, although earthquakes can also occur along "faults" in the crust. A fault is a break in the crust, along which rocks move. When the plates move, cracks or even mountains can result. Earthquakes send out energy as seismic waves, like ripples. The underground point of movement is called the "focus," and above it, on the surface, is the "epicenter" of the movement. The San Andreas fault in California is one of most famous faults in the United States, and the entire Pacific rim is encircled by a series of shifting plates and faults.

When there is a shifting of plates and a fault in the crust, magna can flow through the vent as "lava." A volcano is the opening in the crust from which lava flows. Some volcanoes form in the ocean with plates moving apart or together, and some form when plates move over a hot spot, as with the volcanoes that formed the Hawaiian Islands. There are different types of volcanoes. A "shield" volcano forms large mountains with gentle slopes from runny lava. A "cinder cone" volcano is small with steep sides from thick lava that hardens quickly. A "composite" volcano, a combination of the two, makes a midsized mountain with steep peaks and gently sloping sides. Volcanoes can actually build new land, as in Iceland, which adds acreage yearly from volcanic activity. Volcanoes can also be destrucive: for example, the Caribbean island of Montserrat was evacuated in the 1990s after a series of volcanic eruptions. Generally, the brighter the color, the hotter the lava.

Volcanic mountains are only one of several significant landforms—a particular shape of part of the earth. The three major landforms are plains (large, flat, lowlying areas), plateaus (flat, raised areas that rise steeply from the areas around them), and mountains (highrising peaks). Not only valleys and canyons are formed from those three, but there are various types of plains, plateaus, and mountains created as well. The four main types of mountains are folded, upwarped, faultblock, and volcanic. Folded mountains occur when rock layers are squeezed together from opposite sides by plates in the Earth's crust. Upwarped mountains are formed when crust is pushed up, and faultblock mountains are formed when a large crack in rock results in a block being tilted and pushed up. Finally, volcanic mountains, as noted above, are formed by volcanic lava that piles up into a mountain. Plains and plateaus are flat land that usually has been smoothly sculpted by wind or water erosion, as have canyons, while valleys may be the result of erosion or the movement of glaciers across the land.

Most of the earth is composed of rock, which is hard and non-living, and the "rock cycle" is the name for never-ending rock changes. Rock can be large cliffs and boulders or small grains of sand. Rocks are made of one or more minerals, (diamonds, formed from fossilized carbon, are an exception). A mineral is a solid, non-living material with particles in a natural repeating pattern, and minerals have various kinds and degrees of hardness. Water, natural chemistry, and heat all help form different minerals. Some minerals can be used in natural form, while others must be refined. Some of the main properties of minerals are streak (color when rubbed on a streak plate), luster (shininess or how it reflects light), and hardness (the ability to resist being scratched).

One of the three major types of rock is igneous, which is formed when melted rock (called magma) from below the earth's surface, often from volcanoes, cools and hardens into fine grained rock (such as gneiss and granite). If the rock is slow in cooling, it will be coarser grained. The second type, sedimentary rock (such as limestone), is the result of weathering and erosion, during which layers of deposits come together and are squeezed into rock. The Grand Canyon is a good example of sedimentary rock with twenty layers of sediment viewable.

Finally, metamorphic rocks (such as marble or slate) are formed from other rocks. High temperatures and pressure act on the rocks, which then become metamorphic rocks. Metamorphic rock is igneous or sedimentary rock (or other metamorphic rock) changed by heat and pressure. Water and wind, however, can break up metamorphic rocks into sedimentary rocks.

Rocks are broken down by weathering, and "erosion" is simply movement of the weathered rock and soil. "Creep" is a type of slow erosion, usually sediments slowly working their way down a slope. Gravity is a force of erosion, since it causes such materials to move, and major slippage of materials down a slope is called a "slump." A "delta" is soil deposited at a river mouth by erosion and dropping of sediments by gravity. A "rockslide" is a fast fall of rocks, often caused by winter freezing and thawing, and subsequent rock movement. "Mudflows" occur in dry areas with lots of sediment—when rain falls, gravity causes the heavy mud to slide downhill, but terraces, walls, or plant roots help preserve steep hills from erosion.

Wind erodes rock and soil by blowing small bits, leaving heavier, coarser material behind to form a "desert pavement." Abrasion is caused when blowing sediment strikes rock, scraping and wearing the surface. Abrasion is most common where there are few plants to hold the soil. Sandstorms and dust storms also cause erosion, but windbreaks and roots help stop it. Sediments blown by wind are eventually deposited into several types of landforms, such as loess (fine grained sediment) usually very fertile, and dunes, which occur when a rock or clump of some material blocks blowing sediment.

In an area where it snows a lot and the snow does not melt, the bottom snow gets compressed into ice, and it starts to slide. Glaciers are moving masses of ice and snow that change the land. There are valley glaciers and continental glaciers. Continental glaciers are huge masses, and the periods when they covered most of the earth were known as "ice ages." Valley glaciers are common today in high, cold areas. When glaciers move, they carry trees, earth, and rock along, contributing to erosion, but when they melt, they drop soil ("outwash") and rock ("till"), sometimes in a ridge called a "moraine." A winding ridge of rock and gravel left behind by a glacier is called an "esker."

It can be very difficult to tell the ages of rocks and other non-living things. The "principle of superposition" says that, for undisturbed layers of rock, the oldest rocks are on the bottom and the youngest ones on top, but if the rock has been disturbed through plate activity such as folds, earthquakes, or volcanoes, that principle does not necessarily apply. Relative dating helps use faults, river canyons, or other characteristics to help date the layers of sedimentary rock, but, again, it will not work if the rocks have been disturbed or even turned upside down by plate activity, known as "plate tectonics." Sometimes a layer of rock is even missing, usually because of erosion, a gap known as an "unconformity." Correlating rock layers can be formed far apart by the same mineral deposits, and they are usually examined for similar fossils as well, to try to determine if they are part of one continuous deposit.

Absolute dating is much more complex than relative dating. In absolute dating, scientists measure the time it takes for isotopes in the atoms of the rock to decay, a period known as the "half-life." Through this kind of radiometric dating, and using the principle of "uniformitarianism," which says that processes taking place today are similar to those of the past, scientists have figured that the earth is almost 5 billion years old. Carbon-14 is used for dating once-living things, since after an organism dies, the carbon-14 slowly decays and escapes as gas, so the remaining amount indicates how long the organism has been dead.

FOSSILS

A fossil is the imprint or mineralized remains left of a plant or animal that lived and died long ago. Mud turns into rock, sometimes with a print left in it. Many fossils are found in rocks, where they have turned to stone, or in tar or amber, where the whole animal or plant may be trapped, or even frozen into the ground. Fossils form in sedimentary rocks when a plant or animal is buried quickly by sediment. Trace fossils are fossils such as tracks, burrows, animal holes, or droppings. Fossils can show how a species has changed and what the earth was like in an area, and they can suggest climate. Fossils may provide information about the plant or animal itself or about the environment, as when palm fossils, for example, are found in cold climates, which show that those climates used to be warmer.

Fossil bones are also called "petrified remains," as the original material in the remains have been replaced over time by minerals, so the remains are now hard and rocky. Another type of fossil is the "carbonaceous film," which is a thin layer of carbon left when gas and liquids are forced from the dead organism due to pressure and heat from sediment piled on top of it. Index fossils are the fossils of organisms that have changed relatively quickly over the years, so they help to tell the date of rock layers or other fossils. A "mold" is the shape of a plant or animals left in sediment when the rock is formed, while a "cast" results when mud or minerals fill a mold—both are fossils.

A lot of energy used by humans comes from fossil fuels, created by the decaying remains of once-living plants and animals. It is thought that fossil fuels were formed over millions of years from dead plants and animals covered by deposits of sediments such as sand and mud. The pressure generated heat, which caused chemical reactions, forming oil, coal, and natural gas. Peat, for example, becomes lignite, which becomes bitumen, which becomes anthracite—the most valuable coal as it is almost pure carbon due to age and pressure. Petroleum and natural gas are found only in sedimentary rock, mostly sandstone, so geologists look there for fossil fuel. Many deposits are from the remains of sea life, so some deposits are found either underwater today or in areas formerly under water.

As important as fossil fuels are to humans, those fuels give off gases when burned, creating pollution. Since fossil fuels take so long to be created, they are called "nonrenewable resources" (as opposed, for example, to a "renewable resource" such as wood, which quickly grows again, or an "inexhaustible resource" such as wind, hydroelectric power, or sunlight, which will not run out for billions of years). The movement toward alternative fuels may increase because of concern about what to use for energy when there are no longer any fossil fuels.

SOIL AND LAND BIOMES

Soil is another resource that should also be preserved and protected from pollution and erosion. The practices of overfarming and cutting trees contribute to too much carbon dioxide in the air and to global warming, since the forests make needed oxygen from carbon dioxide, water, and sunlight. Soil provides food and shelter, two important factors for humans.

Topsoil is loose material made of weathered rock, humus (decayed parts of plants and animals), air, and water. Plants grow in topsoil, although subsoil is mostly made of rock. There are thousands of types of soil, from clay to sandy, identifiable by different colors and textures. Clay soils hold water, and sandy soils don't. The type of soil depends on the amounts of humus, clay, silt, and sand it contains. Soil very high in humus is best, since fertile soil grows a lot of plants. A good mixture of minerals and humus is called "loam," and loam is very desirable because plants use minerals from the soil to grow. Compost piles recycle soil nutrients, wind and water can cause erosion, and plants can protect soil from erosion.

Soil conservation methods include strip farming (alternating rows of sod with rows of harvestable crops), terracing (cutting into hills to make flat areas), and contour plowing (plowing at right angles to the slope of the land, so soil and water do not run off). Roots, stones, and retaining walls also help to hold soil in place. Growing the same crop over and over weakens soil by using too much of the same nutrients, so "crop rotation," alternating crops that have different nutritional needs, is very helpful in preserving the soil. Soil conservation is important, since it is estimated that it takes 500 to 1,000 years to create one inch of soil.

George Washington Carver was a strong promoter of both crop rotation and composting, as well as responsible for discovering many uses for legumes such as peanuts, beans, and soybeans, which add needed nitrogen and potassium to the soil. Some Native Americans buried fish as fertilizer, since potassium is found in bone meal. Fertilizers can change soils, and farmers currently use both natural and artificial fertilizers, although there is some controversy about the effects of too much chemical fertilizer.

Land biomes are regions of the earth with similar climates and plant and animal life. There are seven main biomes that can be found in various places around the world, although there is more variety in the Northern Hemisphere, since there is not as much land in the Southern Hemisphere. The biomes are ice, tundra, taiga, temperate deciduous forest, tropical rain forest, grassland, and desert. The first, the ice biome is generally a stark, harsh environment, with little or no plant or animal life.

The second, the tundra, sometimes called a "cold desert," is a dry, treeless region near the North Pole, where the temperatures are so cold the ground remains frozen year around, with only the top few inches of ground thawing and the rest "permafrost." Since the cold slows down decomposition and only reindeer moss, grasses, and small shrubs grow there, the soil is usually poor and thin. The tundra supports a surprising array of animal life, from insects to caribou and musk oxen, including many birds that only spend the summers there.

The third, the taiga, is the world's largest biome, stretching across the northern portions of North America, northern Europe, and northern Asia. It is a cold region of dense evergreen trees that is warmer and wetter than the tundra, with no permafrost. Fourth is the temperate deciduous forest, found in both hemispheres below about fifty degrees latitude. These regions usually have four seasons with precipitation year round, freezing temperatures in the winter, and warm temperatures in the summer. Although there are many coniferous (evergreen) trees, deciduous trees that lose their leaves in the winter are most common, and there is a wide array of other plant and animal life.

Closer to the equator is the tropical rain forest, which thrives in warm, stable temperatures and plenty of rain. Because of its great diversity of habitats, the rain forest generally contains the most species of plants and animals, including thousands of different kinds of insects. The trees are often so big that their high canopies form a whole, separate environment and prevent sunlight from reaching the forest floor. The rain forests are the "lungs" of the earth, since their lush growth provides much of earth's oxygen through plant photosynthesis. In addition, 20 percent of the wood for industry, plus spices, food, medicine, and raw materials come from the rain forests.

Tropical and temperate regions that receive less rain are a sixth kind of biome, called grasslands. They have wet and dry seasons, and many grasses that form sod, but with relatively few trees occurring naturally. The soil is often very fertile, so grasslands are usually very productive farming areas, and they support grazing animals.

The last biome, the desert, can be found in many different parts of the world. It typically receives less than ten inches of rain a year and supports relatively little plant or animal life. Those plants and animals that do live there have made specific adaptations to deal with the desert's harsh conditions, most notably the lack of water. Cactus plants, for example, have waxy, spiny leaves that conserve water, and shallow roots that can quickly absorb the rare rainfall. Many desert plants grow low to the ground with long, shallow roots, thin stems, and spiny leaves. While the desert does not support large animals, even the small ones rarely come out in the heat of the day. Reptiles, small mammals, scorpions, and insects typically live in the desert.

FRESH WATER

There are water biomes, both fresh water and saltwater, as well as land biomes. Freshwater environments are delineated by their low level of salt in the water, and they include lakes, ponds, rivers, and streams. Aside from salt, factors that affect freshwater biomes are oxygen, water temperature, and sunlight. Oxygen is most plentiful in flowing water that mixes in air, since slow or stagnant water has more sediment, higher nutrient levels (with, consequently, more plant growth), and less oxygen. Ponds tend to be shallower and warmer than bigger lakes, so ponds usually have more vegetation. Both are home to microscopic plant and animal organisms known as plankton, but very little plant life lives at the bottom of cold, deep lakes, since the sun's rays do not usually reach there.

Fresh water is a valuable resource. Although about 70 percent of the earth's surface is covered by water, which is needed to keep living things alive, only about 3 percent of the water on earth is fresh water, with three-quarters of that frozen as glaciers or as icecaps near the poles. Less than 1 percent of the water found on earth is available fresh water. Surface water mostly comes from precipitation, like rain or snow, that condenses in the atmosphere and falls to earth. Surface water is easily seen in lakes, ponds, streams, and rivers. Fresh water that collects underground is called "groundwater" and is used for wells.

Groundwater collects in spaces, called pores, beneath the ground, which is considered permeable if there are lots of connected pore spaces so water can move easily through soil and rock, and considered impermeable if the ground is made of rock and hard clay that water cannot pass through. Usually there is an impermeable layer under permeable soil and rock. If water fills up a lot of pores until the ground is saturated, it forms an "aquifer," an underground pool of water, and the upper surface of that water is called the "water table."

People drill wells in the ground to pump groundwater for drinking. However, if there is not enough rain to continually refill the aquifer, the wells can run dry. An artesian well rarely runs dry, but it is much more expensive to drill, because it must be drilled deeply in a sloping aquifer between two impermeable layers, so gravity-pressurized water will flow to the surface.

Water forms a spring where the water table is at the earth's surface. Springs can be either cold or, more rarely, hot, if the groundwater has been heated by rocks heated from molten material. In some cases, the spring is a "geyser," meaning the water is heated so hot that it periodically shoots out of the ground and releases steam. Sometimes, water mixes with carbon dioxide in the air and becomes acidic, cutting through soft rock and forming underground caves, and often leaving rock formations sticking up from the floor (stalagmites) or hanging from the ceiling (stalactites), depending on the pattern of the dripping. If the cave roof collapses, causing the ground above to fall in, the hole is called a sinkhole.

Water that does not soak into the ground or evaporate is called runoff—it runs along the ground and eventually enters streams, lakes, or the ocean. The amount and length of time rain falls affect runoff and the rate of soaking in, as do the slope of land, the number of plants, and the amount of pavement. "Rill erosion" occurs when a small stream forms during a heavy rain. In "gully erosion," a rill channel becomes broader and deeper to form a gully. "Sheet erosion" occurs when rainwater flows into lower elevations carrying sediment with it, and at the lower elevations the water loses some of its energy and drains into soil or slowly evaporates. "Stream erosion" refers to water in a stream picking up sediment and carrying it, continuously cutting a deeper and wider channel.

It is important that neither surface water nor groundwater become polluted, which happens when harmful chemicals or biological materials are added to the water. If the source of the pollution is identifiable, it is called the "point source" and is relatively easy to stop or to clean up, but much pollution comes from "nonpoint sources" such as fertilizer runoff, oil drippings, or leaky sewage, which may be hard to find or stop. Proper disposal of poisons and other harmful substances, such as used oil and paint (they should not be poured down the drain), is important in curbing pollution and keeping water clean.

There are three kinds of streams. The first kind is narrow and fast, with a high level of energy and, consequently, a lot of erosion on the bottom. These are considered "young streams," no matter how old they are. The second kind, "mature streams," are wider and slower, with more side erosion, which forms curves, known as meanders. The valley floor formed by a meandering stream is called a floodplain. The third kind of stream is the "old stream" that flows slowly through its floodplain. The term "floodplain" indicates that a large amount of water covers normally dry land from time to time.

The point where these various kinds of streams meet is a river. Streams drain into rivers that drain into lakes or oceans, and the area drained by several rivers is known as a drainage basin, or watershed. Parts of the drainage basin may sometimes flood, especially on the floodplain when there is too much water from rain or snow. River water carries sediment, small bits of dirt and rock, and drops the sediment when the water slows down—often at the mouth of the river where it empties into a larger body of water, such as a big lake, a gulf, or an ocean. The land built up by the sediment deposits is called a "delta," and deltas often form in "estuaries," where salt and fresh water meet and mix, such as in the Chesapeake Bay, the lower part of the Everglades, or where the Mississippi River meets the Gulf of Mexico.

OCEANS

Oceans cover about three-quarters of the earth and contain about 97 percent of the earth's water. It is thought that oceans were formed when water vapor stored in the earth's atmosphere began to condense into clouds and rain, and ocean were formed in low areas called "basins." It has recently been discovered that the oceans are natural air cleansers— the coarse sea salt in the ocean spray encourages rain that washes dust and other pollutants out of the atmosphere, so polluted air is cleaned when it passes from being over land to being over the ocean.

Oceans are salty because they contain the residue from all the fresh water that ever ran into them, including many minerals that have leached out of rocks over millions of years, and chemicals such as sodium, calcium, magnesium, and chlorine (which mostly appears as gas from volcanoes). High salt content is also a characteristic of a few inland seas and lakes, such as the Dead Sea and Great Salt Lake. The oceans appear to be stable and not growing saltier, because as new elements are added to the oceans, others are removed through sediment and biological processes of sea animals, as when calcium, for example, forms shells for some animals.

People also, of course, eat ocean fish and shellfish, as well as sea plants, and they use carrageenin (a kind of seaweed) in making commercial ice cream. It is possible to remove the salt from ocean water, a process known as desalination, and doing so makes the water drinkable for humans. However, it is a complicated process that includes evaporating the sea water and collecting the fresh water as it condenses, so it is relatively expensive and not very common. In addition to vast amounts of animal and plant life, the ocean also has rich deposits of minerals called "placer deposits." These are common where rivers enter the ocean. Gas, oil, nickel, manganese, and cobalt are also extracted from the ocean, as is much of the table salt used by humans.

The ocean floor has major geographic features, including the highest mountains and the deepest valleys on earth. The shoreline is located wherever the ocean meets the land, and beyond that, towards the sea, is a gradual downward slope known as the "continental shelf," the underwater edge of the continent. The continental shelf runs into the "continental slope," which is steeper than the continental shelf and runs down to the ocean floor, where the mountains, valleys, and plains of the ocean basin are located.

As deposits are dropped in the ocean floor, flat areas called "abyssal plains" are created deep below the ocean surface. Plate movements in the earth's crust also occur on the ocean floor, creating ridges and volcanoes. Lava from the volcanoes cools in the water, adding new layers of rock to the ocean floor. Where the volcanoes are high enough to stick out of the ocean, they form islands, as in Hawaii. Crustal plates often form trenches where they meet, and most ocean trenches are much larger than comparable valleys on land. The Marianas Trench, found in the Pacific, as are most deep trenches, is thought to be the deepest place on the earth.

CURRENTS, TIDES, AND WAVES

Oceans move in currents, which are like rivers of water flowing within the ocean. "Surface currents" are currents in the top layers of the ocean, and they are caused by prevailing winds, and can carry cold water to warm regions or warm water to cold regions, moving water parallel to the earth's surface. Surface currents are caused by wind patterns and by the "Coriolis effect," which is caused by the rotation of the earth. The Coriolis effect causes wind to turn (clockwise in the northern hemisphere, counterclockwise in the Southern hemisphere), affecting the surface currents caused by the wind.

One of the most famous currents is the Gulf Stream, which moves water north along the East Coast from Florida and across the Atlantic to northern Europe. The Gulf Stream moderates the climate of the British Isles, despite their location so far north, by bringing warm water from areas around the equator. The continents also affect the ocean currents, which change their direction when they encounter these huge land masses. Sometimes, too, climate is affected by "upwelling," which is a circulation in the ocean that brings deep cold water to the surface, making the nearby land colder.

Another type of current is the "deep ocean" or "density" current, which forms when cold, dense seawater sinks below warmer, less heavy water (since cold water is heavier than warm water), and which circulates ocean water slowly. The density of seawater can be affected by the amount of salinity or by a change in temperature, but dense waters move very slowly and may take hundreds of years to reach the surface and to affect climate. When waves hit the shore at an angle, they create a "longshore current," which carries lots of sediment, a sort of river of sand. Shoreline currents are local currents that run along the coast, while "rip currents" are shoreline currents that flow away from the beach, their direction is often caused by a sand spit. A "longshore current" is caused by waves that strike the shore at an angle and move water forward along the shore, carrying lots of sedimentation.

The tides are daily changes in water levels of the ocean locally, based on the gravitational cycle of the moon, which exerts a strong pull of gravity on the earth. The sun also affects the tides, and when the earth, moon, and sun are lined up in a row, their combined gravity forms high tides known as "spring tides." Alternatively, when they form a right angle, their lesser gravity forms "neap tides," which are lower. Tides form a bulge on the side nearest the moon (where gravity is strongest) and another bulge on the directly opposite side of the earth (where gravity is weakest). Tidal power can be very strong, and people have built dams and electric plants to harness that power, although tidal dams can cause environmental problems.

A wave is an up and down movement of water particles. The strength of a wave depends on the strength of the wind, the amount of time wind blows, and the size of area. Waves can cause erosion and drop sediment, a process known as "deposition." Most ocean waves are caused by wind, but earthquakes and volcanoes can cause "tsunamis"—giant waves. Extremely low pressure can also cause waves. During hurricanes, large domes of water called "storm surges" form because low pressure at the storm's center causes ocean water to rise. Strong winds form huge waves on top of the storm surge and push this high water ahead of the storm. Another type of huge wave is the "rogue wave," which forms when large storm waves join together.

The shoreline is where the ocean and the land meet, and waves and currents can change the shoreline. Along the shores of the oceans, sediment is constantly being deposited and picked up, mostly from currents, tides, and waves. Some shorelines are steep and rocky, while others have great deposits of sediment that have formed sand beaches and tidal pools—scooped out sand basins that are under water at high tide. Beaches can be different colors and textures, depending on the kind of rock from which the sand was formed. Barrier islands, as well as beaches, are sand ridges formed by breaking waves, then sculpted by the wind into dunes. Barrier islands tend to be ecologically fragile, and often do not last very long.

OCEAN LIFE

The main saltwater biome is, of course, the oceans, which are divided into the lighted zone, where sunlight can penetrate, and the dark zone, where it cannot. Most of the many varieties of plants, animals, and algae that live in the ocean, live in the "light zone" of the continental shelf, where sun can penetrate, and plants, like the forests of kelp that grow there, can form food. Few animals live in the dark zone because there is also a scarcity of plant life.

The areas where rivers flow into the oceans are called estuaries, and they are a mix of fresh and salt water. Estuaries are extremely fertile, as they have nutrients pouring from the river, and often are rich areas for fish and for shellfish such as clams, shrimp, and oysters. Along the estuaries and the rest of the oceans' edges are "intertidal zones"—the part of the shoreline that is covered with water at high tide and exposed to the air at low tide. Organisms living there must be adaptable to changes in water level, temperature, and wave action.

All life on earth is water based, and it is thought that life began in the oceans. However, some organisms have adapted to living on land and some to living under water. The sun gives off radiant energy that is captured by chlorophyll-containing ocean plants to make food through the process of photosynthesis. Tiny organisms, such as krill (animals) and plankton (one-celled algae, plants, or animals), consume the food, and are themselves consumed by other animals (mostly bottom dwellers, known as "benthos," and animals that swim, known as "nekton"), right up the food chain to giant sharks. Multiple food chains are called food webs, which are very complex and interconnected.

Coral reefs occur in underwater tropical climates of warm salty water, and are made up of rocky skeletons of tiny organisms called "corals," which live in one place on algae and build limestone skeletons around their bodies by taking calcium out of seawater. These coral bodies form reefs, and many other animals find shelter in them. Thousands of other species, including sponges, shellfish, and fish, live in coral reefs. Because sea water tends to have a stable temperature, sea organisms do not have to adapt to much change in environment. Ocean plants and animals reproduce in various ways, and they get their food either through photosynthesis, through filtering water to get nutrients, or through moving around to find it.

READINGS FOR STUDENTS

Aulenbach, N. and Barton, H. (2001). *Exploring Caves: Journeys into the Earth*. Washington D. C.: National Geographic Society.

Bial, R. (2000). *A Handful of Dirt*. New York: Walker.

Cone, M. (1997). *Squishy, Misty, Damp & Muddy: The In-between World of Wetlands*. San Francisco: Sierra Club.

Dewy, J. (2001). *Antarctic Journal: Four Months at the Bottom of the World*. New York: HarperCollins Children's Books.

Downs, S. (2000). *Earth's Fiery Fury*. Brookfield, CT: Twenty-First Century Books/Millbrook Press.

DuTemple, L. (2000). *Jacques Cousteau*. Minneapolis: Lerner Publications.

Earle, S. (1999). *Dive! My Adventures in the Deep Frontier*. Washington D.C.: National Geographic.

Glaser, L. (1997). *Compost! Growing Gardens from Your Garbage*. Brookfield, CT: Millbrook Press.

Glaser, L. (2000). *Our Big Home: An Earth Poem*. Brookfield. CT: Millbrook Press.

Hiscock, B. (1998). *The Big Rivers: The Missouri, the Mississippi, and the Ohio*. New York: Atheneum.

Holmes, T. (1998). *Fossil Feud: Rivalry of the First American Dinosaur Hunters*. New York: Messner.

Ingoglia, G. (1991). *Look Inside the Earth*. New York: Putnam.

Johnson, R. (1996). *Science on the Ice: An Antarctic Journal*. Minneapolis: Lerner.

Kramer, S. (1996). *Caves*. Minneapolis: Carolrhoda.

Lambert, D. (1998). *The Kingfisher Young People's Book of Oceans*. New York: Kingfisher.

Lampton, C. (1991). *Earthquake*. Brookfield, CT: Millbrook Press.

Lauber, P. (1991). *Volcanoes and Earthquakes*. New York: Scholastic.

Lye, K. (1991). *The Earth*. Brookfield, CT: Millbrook Press.

Malam, J. (1997). *Highest, Longest, Deepest: A Foldout Guide to the World's Record Breakers*. New York: Simon and Schuster.

National Geographic. (2001). *National Geographic Student Atlas of the World*. Washington D.C.: National Geographic Society.

Oldfield, S. (1997). *Rain Forests*. Minneapolis: Lerner.

Pope, J. (1996). *The Children's Atlas of Natural Wonders*. Brookfield, CT: Millbrook Press.

Ross, M. (2000). *Exploring the Earth with John Welsey Powell*. Minneapolis: Carolrhoda Books/Lerner.

Sattler, H. (1996). *Our Patchwork Planet*. New York: Lothrop.

Schwartz, L. (1991). *My Earth Book*. Learning Works.

Sussman, A. (2000). *Dr. Art's Guide to Planet Earth: For Earthlings Ages 12 to 120*. White River Junction, VT: Chelsea Green.

Tagliaferro, L. (2001). *Galapagos Islands: Nature's Delicate Balance at Risk*. Minneapolis: Lerner Publications.

Walker, S. (1997). *Earthquakes*. Minneapolis: Carolrhoda.

Winner, S. (1999). *Erosion (Carolrhoda Earth Watch Book Series)*. Minneapolis: Carolrhoda/Lerner.

WEBSITES

StudyWorks! Online: Earth Science Links
www.studyworksonline.com/cda/content/explorations/

Instructional Materials for Science Educators
www.ncsu.edu/sciencejunctin/terminal/imse/lowres/2/imseinfo.htm

Teacher Links
edcdaac.usgs.gov/education/teacher_links.html

Earth/Space Sciences
www.thejournal.com/features/rdmap/hs128c.cfm

Lesson Plans
www.theteacherscorner.net/science/earth/index.htm

Earth and Oceans
www.geo.arizona.edu/geo2xx/geo212/01/tsld005.htm

Athena Classroom Projects
learn.arc.nasa.gov/products/products01/ltp_html/individual_pages/
athena.html

NASA's Learning Technologies Project
learn.arc.nasa.gov/features/1999/athena_feat/athena_feat.html

Star's & Space @ Morgan's Kids World—WebWorld—1000's of links
discover-net.net/~mlana/morthestars.html

Origin of Earth, Oceans, and Life
wwwcatsic.ucsc.edu/~eart1/Notes/Lec1.html

Earth and Ocean Sciences
web.uvic.ca/calendar2001/GRAD/GPROGS/EaOcS/

Spacelink—CAMEX
spacelink.nasa.gov/NASA.Projects/Earth.Science/Atmosphere/CAMEX/

Origins of Earth and Oceans
www.personal.kent.edu/~dwitter/oce/s2002/lecture-notes/origins/
origins-lec.htm

Nicholas School—Division of Earth and Ocean Sciences
www.env.duke.edu/eos/programs/undergrad/couseprogressions.html

Math and Science of Earth System Science
www.unidata.ucar.edu/staff/blynds/tiereport.html

UVic: Earth and Ocean Sciences Programs
web.uvic.ca/calendar2001/FACS/FoSc/SoEaaOS/EaOcSP.html

The Gateway to Educational Materials
www.thegateway.org/keywords/e.html

Tides
www.cofc.edu/CGOinquiry/tides.htm

School District of the City of Royal Oak—Science Links
www.rosd.k12.mi.us/links/science-links.html

The River Continuum
www.oaa.pdx.edu/CAE/Programs/sti/pratt/hydrology.html

Science & the Internet
oops.bizland.com/sciencenet.htm

Library Media/Science
chesterfield.k12.va.us/Instruction/Library_Media/MS/science.html

My Favorite Links
www.anzwers.org/free/geolor/My%20Favorite%20Links_educational%20
resources.htm

Science Education Resources
www.sau3.org/bhs/sciencelink.htm

■ ■ ■ ■ ■ ━━━━━━━━━━━━━━━━━━━━━━━━━━━━━━━━━━

CHAPTER 6

SPACE, WEATHER, AND CLIMATE

SPACE

The universe is everything that exists in space, including planets, stars, dust, gases, and energy, however, most of the universe is empty. The solar system consists of the earth's sun and the objects that orbit it. A planet is a large body of rock or gas that orbits a sun, and the greater the planet's mass, the greater its pull of gravity. A satellite is any body that orbits another, so the planets are satellites of the sun, and the moons are satellites of the planets. In their order from the sun, the nine planets of our sun's solar system are Mercury, Venus, Earth, Mars, Jupiter, Saturn, Uranus, Neptune, and Pluto. The four inner planets are smaller and warmer than the five outer planets, which, except for Pluto (which is small and made of rock), are very large. Jupiter is the largest planet and has an ongoing circular storm known as the "Great Red Spot," and Saturn is known for its rings. Those four large, outer planets are called "gas giants" because they are made of frozen gases. All five of the outer planets are very cold. Earth is the only planet with a watery surface and a lot of oxygen, so it is the only planet that supports plant and animal life, although there is evidence that water may have once existed on Mars or Venus. Because they are made of rock or frozen gas, planets do not appear to twinkle in the atmosphere, as do stars.

The earth travels through space at 67,000 miles per hour and spins in rotation once every 24 hours, which causes day and night. The earth also circles the sun in an elliptical orbit, one revolution every 365 and one-quarter days. For part of the year, the North Pole tilts in the direction of the sun, so it is summer in the northern hemisphere and the South Pole tilts away, so it is winter in the southern hemisphere.

Moons are large, rock objects that orbit planets. Earth has one moon and Mars two, while the other inner planets have none. Pluto has one moon, and the other outer planets have multiple moons. Asteroids are smaller, revolving chunks of rock, also part of the solar system, and a major astroid belt lies between Mars and Jupiter.

The earth's moon was originally molten rock, and it cooled into craters, mountains, and plains, originally thought to be oceans but now known to be hardened lava. The moon has no atmosphere or wind, and no water, so consequently it has very little erosion. "Phases" are different shapes the moon appears to have, depending on the angle of light it receives from the sun. A lunar eclipse occurs when the earth's shadow falls on the moon, throwing it into darkness. By contrast, a solar eclipse occurs when the moon's shadow falls on the earth, throwing it into darkness.

The earth's moon looks like the largest object in the night sky: stars and other planets actually are much bigger, but look smaller as they are so far away. The moon is the closest natural satellite to the earth, which it orbits every twenty-nine days, and the moon's light is a reflection from the sun. From the earth, people see only the portions of the moon lit by sun, so it looks as though the moon changes over the twenty-nine days.

The sun, 93 million miles away, is the star closest to the earth and is at the center of the solar system. The sun is a hot ball of glowing gases, about 25 million degrees Fahrenheit, that shines all the time, so darkness only occurs on the part of the earth facing away from the sun at any given time. The sun does not move, but because the earth does, it looks as though the sun moves.

The sun is almost 870,000 miles in diameter. Its hot gases give off light and heat known as "solar energy," which is used by most things on earth. As particles of hydrogen smash into each other under pressure and produce helium, the sun releases energy as light and heat in a process called "fusion" (because the hydrogen particles fuse, or join together, to form helium).

The sun is the source of all energy in our atmosphere, and it reaches the earth through radiation—the transfer of energy by electromagnetic waves. Direct contact with something warm passes heat to the cooler object through conduction—the transfer of energy when molecules bump into one another. Convection is the transfer of heat by the flow of a heated material. The sun consists of a core at its center, which makes up most of its mass, then a "radiation zone." Energy heats this layer and moves to the outer layer, the "convection zone," in which energy moves to the surface as cooler particles are pulled down by gravity, pushing warmer particles up. The surface of the sun, the "photosphere" or "sphere of light," is the part seen from earth, and beyond that is the "corona," an area of hot gases that extends out over a half million miles.

"Sunspots" are dark spots that are cooler than the rest of the photosphere, and that grow and shrink in number as "sunspot cycles." Sunspots produce solar flares and solar prominences—brief bursts of energy from the photosphere, made up of ultraviolet waves, radio waves, and x-rays. Sunspots are cooler and less light than prominences, which are fountains—both are temporary. Bits of gases called "solar wind" are thrown into space, and the particles can cause magnetic storms when they reach the earth.

The sun looks very bright from the earth because how bright a star looks depends not only upon how bright it actually is, but also upon its distance from the earth. Like the sun, the other stars do not move individually (although there is movement in the universe, such as the Milky Way rotating), but seem to because the earth moves. "Apparent magnitude" (how bright the star looks) may be different from "absolute magnitude" (how bright it actually is). The "main sequence" is a band formed by classifying stars, based on their absolute magnitude, surface temperature, color, and size. Most stars are classified as main sequence stars. Depending on the location in the main sequence, it is possible to figure out important information about the star.

Stars are thought to begin their lives as "nebulae" within huge clouds of dust, hydrogen, and helium, as gravity pulls the particles together over millions of years. Stars form and give off gases when they become hot enough, and the gases in the nebulae shine and glow different colors—hydrogen glows red, and oxygen and helium glow green. Thus, stars can be different sizes or colors, with larger stars generally being cooler. The color of a star can be a clue, as red stars are the coolest, yellow ones are medium, and bluish-white are the hottest. A comet is a traveling ball of ice and dust, in which the ice forms glowing gases as it gets nearer the sun, making a long, bright tail. A "shooting star," by contrast, is actually a meteor, a rock that breaks out of its orbit in space and burns upon entry into the earth's atmosphere.

As a star grows in mass and becomes a "protostar," its temperature rises and it begins to glow, producing energy (which is what makes it a star). Next, it becomes a main sequence star, when the temperature is hot enough for various kinds of energy to be released. The star shines until its hydrogen runs low, then the star begins to expand, growing to as much as 100 times its original size, becoming a "red giant."

In billions of years, when the sun expands into a red giant, it is expected that it will burn up Mercury and Venus, and that the earth will become too hot to support life. If the core of a supergiant collapses, the outer part of the star explodes and shines very brightly for a few days, an event known as a "supernova." What is left of the star becomes a "white dwarf," which shines on dimly as it slowly cools. When the rest of the gases are gone, the star shrinks to become a "black dwarf," or, if it was a supergiant, the core is called a "neutron star," and may become a black hole if the core is big enough.

A galaxy is a cluster of stars held together by gravity. Galaxies can be either elliptical, spiral, or irregular, although elliptical are the most common. The ribbon of stars overhead indicates the center of the earth's galaxy, known as the Milky Way. It includes more than 100 billion stars and is one of the largest galaxies in the universe.

There are four kinds of galaxies, spiral, barred spiral, elliptical, and irregular. The Milky Way is a spiral galaxy, with the earth's solar system in one of the spiral arms. A spiral galaxy has a thick bulge of older stars in the center, and younger stars, dust, and gas in the arms. A barred spiral galaxy is similar, but the spirals extend from a bar of stars that stretches from the center. Elliptical galaxies can range from almost round to elliptical, and irregular galaxies have no particular pattern.

A "galactic cluster" is a group of galaxies. The Milky Way is one of thirty galaxies in a cluster called the "Local Group." There are many galaxies because the universe is so large. Other galactic clusters are huge, with thousands of clusters, and the distances between them are measured in "light-years." A light-year is the distance light travels in a year—about 5.8 trillion miles.

From earliest human history, there are records of people examining the skies and wanting to know more about space. The Mayans, for example, had observatories in Central America, as did the Greeks in the Mediterranean. The ancients imagined that some stars form outlines, called "constellations," that looked like objects, mythical characters, or animals. There are eighty-eight constellations, and most of their names come from ancient Greek mythology or Native American legend, though different ancients named different constellations. Since the North Star is always in the same place above North Pole, it has been used since before recorded history for navigation (the Southern Cross is the main marker in the southern hemisphere).

Telescopes are used for seeing distant objects, and are often used in observatories—where scientists study planets, stars, the sun, and other aspects of astronomy. In the early 1600s, Galileo Galilei used a telescope with 20–30 magnification to observe mountains on the moon, sunspots, phases of Venus, and the moons around Jupiter. There are two types of telescopes, radio and optical. Optical telescopes can be either refracting or reflecting—refracting telescopes use lenses to magnify objects, and reflecting telescopes magnify objects with curved mirrors. Most telescopes are reflecting telescopes. Radio telescopes collect and focus various types of invisible energy waves, such as radio waves and x-rays, since the kinds of waves absorbed or given off by a star can help indicate what it is made of. Computers can process the data, then use it to create pictures. The most famous space-based telescope is the Hubbell Space Telescope, launched in 1990, which uses cameras to save images and send them back to earth.

In 1957 the Soviet Union launched Sputnik I, and the space race was on. The first person in space was the Russian astronaut Yuri Gagarin in 1961. Later that year, the Mercury program sent the first American into space, and, with Apollo 11, the United States landed Neil Armstrong and Edwin "Buzz" Aldrin, the first people on the moon, on July 16, 1969. There were five more moon missions until the Apollo program ended in 1972.

Later, Viking I and II both landed on Mars in 1976, and Pioneer was sent to Venus. Viking and Pioneer were space probes—robot vehicles used to explore space where it is too dangerous or distant for people to go. Probes carry cameras and other instruments to gather data and send it back to earth. Voyagers 1 and 2 left for space in 1977, sending back photos and data of Jupiter, Saturn, Uranus, and Neptune. Because they give information about such distant places, the Voyagers are considered the greatest achievement thus far in exploring the solar system. Closer to home, space shuttles, which are launched, but land conventionally, have been used and reused since 1981. The successes of the U.S. space program have been marred by three tragedies: Apollo I burned in 1967, killing its three crew members; Challenger exploded in 1986, killing its seven crew members; and Columbia burned on reentry in 2003, killing its seven crew members. Mir was the original Russian space station, and the cooperative building of an International Space Station began in 1998.

WEATHER

Weather occurs in the atmosphere—the air that surrounds the earth. The earth's atmosphere is a mixture of gases, mostly nitrogen and oxygen, with some solids (often pollution, dust, salt, and ice) and liquids (often water) suspended in them. About four-fifths of the atmosphere is nitrogen, and about one-fifth is oxygen, carbon dioxide, and water. The atmosphere is more than one hundred miles thick, but weather only affects the lower six miles. It is made up of layers based on temperature differences, and some layers have gases that hold heat better than others. The part of the atmosphere that is nearest to the earth is the "troposphere," which contains most of the gases and solids, and it is where most of the weather occurs. The troposphere is warmer near the bottom. For example, temperatures usually grow colder as one climbs a mountain, since the air gets thinner and less dense, so it holds less heat.

The next layer up is the "stratosphere," which contains ozone (oxygen with an extra atom to each molecule) that absorbs and holds the sun's radiation and heat, making that layer quite warm (but not as warm as the troposphere), and shielding the earth from harmful ultraviolet radiation. Unfortunately, the ozone layer is shrinking and developing holes, especially over the North and South Poles, and it is thought that pollution is contributing to that situation. Chlorofluorocarbons, airborne chemicals used in the past in many products like hairspray and air conditioner coolant, are thought to be particular culprits, and their use is now restricted in most countries.

The "mesosphere," the next layer, is usually well below freezing. The layer farthest from the earth is the "thermosphere," which is divided into the "ionosphere," a layer of electrically charged particles that help with radio transmissions, and the "exosphere," where, oddly enough, temperatures are very hot because air particles are so far apart. There are fewer molecules and the air pressure is less at the top because as the weight of the gases at the top of the atmosphere presses down, the air close to earth is the densest, so the air pressure is the greatest there.

Weather refers to the current state of the atmosphere, what the air is like outside—temperature, moisture, wind, and air pressure. Weather stations, planes, balloons, and satellites are all used to predict weather, and weather maps show weather for large areas. Temperature is measured with a thermometer, usually either Celsius, in most of the world, or Fahrenheit, in the United States. Temperature changes throughout the day and night and is generally colder at night, since the part of the earth facing away from the sun is not receiving the sun's rays and warmth.

"Precipitation" refers to moisture, in the form of rain, snow, sleet, or hail, falling from the air. The "water cycle" provides the basis for most weather, with the additional interaction of heated air, water, and the sun. The phrase refers to the following process: the sun warms water and air; water evaporates into water vapor in the air, which acts like a sponge; then meets cooler air in the atmosphere and condenses to form clouds, tiny drops of water which join and get heavier, then fall to earth; and the process begins all over again. The amount of water vapor held in the air is known as "humidity," and it is linked to the temperature, since cooler temperatures hold fewer water molecules and allow them to condense, because they are not moving as quickly.

Clouds are an integral part of the water cycle. There are three main types of clouds, stratus (low, gray layers that stretch across the sky), cirrus (high, thin, feathery wisps containing ice crystals), and cumulus (big, fat, puffy collections of water molecules). These three main types of clouds can all be associated with both clear and rainy weather. In addition, "nimbus clouds" are any big clouds so full and dark with water that no sunlight passes through them. The name nimbus can be applied to either cumulus clouds (cumulonimbus) or stratus clouds (nimbostratus) to indicate rain. There are also ways to combine labels to indicate whether particular clouds are high or low in the sky: cirro (high), alto (middle height), and strato (low clouds).

If the air is below freezing when the water changes from a vapor to a liquid in a cloud, several things can happen. The water can become solid instead of liquid, making snow; melt and refreeze near the ground, making sleet; or freeze multiple times around a ball of ice as it is tossed around the atmosphere, making hail. The more water in the air, the higher the "relative humidity," which is a measure of the amount of water the air is holding, compared to the maximum amount it can hold at that specific temperature.

Warmer air in general has fewer molecules than denser cold air, which is usually more high pressure, so high or low pressure is an important indicator for weather. Temperature, density of air, and amount of water vapor all contribute to the atmospheric pressure, which is measured with a barometer. High pressure generally means clear skies and weather, while low pressure systems, which form along the boundaries of air masses, usually mean cloudy skies and sometimes rain.

A large body of air with the same temperature and moisture is called an "air mass." When two air masses of different temperatures meet, they do not usually mix, but form a "front." Warm fronts often produce widespread rain, while cold fronts may produce narrower, more intense storms. A front that stops is called a "stationary front" and precipitation resulting from it can cause blizzards or floods.

Thunderstorms are created when warm, moist air moves upward rapidly, cools, then condenses, forming "cumulonimbus" clouds. Water droplets and ice form and begin falling the long distance toward the earth, getting bigger as they encounter other droplets and dragging the air down with them, causing strong winds. The lightning is produced when a fast uplift of air builds up electric charges in clouds with both positive and negative charges, so when current flows between them, lightning flashes. Thunder is created from the rapid heating of the air around a bolt of lightning, which causes the air to expand quickly, then cool and contract, and the fast movement of the molecules forms sound waves heard as thunder. Some very severe thunderstorms, with winds blowing in different directions at different speeds, form funnel-shaped clouds, called "tornadoes" when they touch the earth. Tornadoes are whirling winds that move in a narrow path over land, picking up dirt and debris, which gives them their dark color. Tornadoes can lift animals, cars, and houses, and can blow out walls and roofs, even though they only last a few minutes.

Wind is another element of weather. Although air takes up space and has weight and pressure, it cannot be seen, tasted, or smelled. Wind is moving air, and a person can feel and see the result of wind, especially in a hurricane or tornado. Wind can even do work, as when windmills and sails are used to harness energy. Wind is caused by the uneven heating of the earth and its atmosphere, which causes areas of pressure differences, and a general circulation of air. Thus, wind is the movement of air from either an area of high pressure or an area of lower pressure. Cold air comes from the North and South Poles, which receive less direct sun rays, making their air colder.

The rotation of the earth creates the "Coriolis effect," which changes the direction of all free-moving objects to the northeast of the equator and to the southwest of the equator, creating wind patterns on the earth's surface. Surface winds and high altitude winds influence daily and seasonal winds. Sea breezes are created when solar radiation warms the land more than the water, creating a current as cooler, denser air moves inland from the ocean. At night, the land cools more quickly than does the ocean, so air over the land becomes cooler than air over the ocean, and the cool, dense air from the land moves out over the water, pushing the warm air over the water upward. These breezes can change with the seasons, forming monsoons or hurricanes—storms with heavy rain and fast winds during certain times of the year.

Powerful hurricanes arise from large, swirling, low-pressure systems that form over tropical oceans, where warm, moist air rises and provides energy for the storms. Hurricanes turn heat energy into wind, bringing high winds and waves, heavy rain, and even tornadoes, but gradually losing power as they pass over land. In the United States, hurricanes are most common near the Gulf of Mexico and the lower East Coast.

Predicting the path of hurricanes and other storms is becoming increasingly accurate, as meteorologists make observations and measure data for weather maps, while satellites provide much more data. Additionally, storms can be tracked by Doppler radar, which sends out radio waves to track the direction in which a storm is moving, so people can be warned to seek shelter. The radar even shows two kinds of winds moving in different directions, indicative of a funnel cloud, and anemometers measure wind speed.

CLIMATE

The four seasons are often what people have in mind when they refer to climate. Seasons are caused by the tilt of the earth when it orbits—if the earth had no tilt, the seasons would always be the same in any given place. The earth moves in an orbit path around the sun during the year, and as it orbits, seasons change. The earth always tilts toward one side so part of the earth faces the sun directly and gets more direct light. When the earth moves to the other side of the sun, that same part of earth faces the sun on a slant and gets less direct light, which both travels and is filtered through more atmosphere. Summer is the time when an area gets the most sun, has the most daylight, and has the warmest temperature. Fall is the time when the tilt of the earth is away, so the area gets less direct sun and, consequently, less daylight and cooler temperatures (this is the time of year when deciduous leaves fall and animals store food for the winter). Winter is the time of year when the rays of the sun are farthest from the particular area, which as a result, gets the least direct sun rays and, consequently, the least daylight hours and the coldest temperatures. Winter is also the time that many plants rest and animals hibernate or live off stored food. Finally, spring is the time when the earth tilts so that the area starts to receive more sun, bringing increasing direct rays and increasing daylight and warmth, so leaves begin to grow and animals come out of hibernation. The seasons, because they are based on which portion of the earth is tilted toward the sun, are opposite in the northern and southern hemispheres, i.e., it is summer in the southern hemisphere when it is winter in the northern hemisphere.

Climate actually is a wider version of weather. It is the general, average pattern of all weather conditions through all seasons that an area has over a span of many years, taking into account average temperature, sunshine, precipitation, air pressure, and humidity. A microclimate is the climate of a very small area that may be sheltered or exposed more than the area around it. Other factors that affect climate include the following: presence or absence of large bodies of water (which usually moderate climate to be warmer in the winter and cooler in the summer, since water is slower than land to cool off or heat up); certain landforms (such as mountains, since higher evevations are usually cooler and mountains often prompt rain); distance from the equator (which affects how much direct sunlight the area receives); and patterns of wind, air masses, and ocean currents. Prevailing winds and ocean currents can also affect and change climate. Global warming can affect climate, and, by contrast, former ice ages have left continental glaciers that still remain in Greenland, the Arctic, and Antarctica.

The United States has many different climates, from northern Alaska to Puerto Rico, but most of the country is temperate—warm in summer and cold in winter. The eastern United States generally gets more rain than does the western part of the country, affecting forests and grasslands, and even desert.

Climate is classified into six categories and further divided into types, or zones. A "climate zone" is a region with similar yearly patterns of rain, temperature, and sunlight. The six zones are: tropical (wet and dry); mild (marine west coast, Mediterranean, and humid subtropical); dry (semiarid and arid); continental (warm summer, cool summer, and subarctic); polar (tundra and ice cap); and high elevation (highlands and uplands). Each of the continents has many different types of climate, as do large countries, such as the United States, that cover a lot of area.

The type of climate of an area determines the vegetation and animal life found there, since all organisms have adaptations that let them thrive in some climates and wither in others. One notable behavioral adaptation is hibernation, common to animals who live where winters are cold. Another is desert animals who obtain moisture from their food, rather than directly from streams or ponds. People have shown themselves to be adaptable to almost every climate, since they live in most parts of the world, even the polar regions.

Most temperature is determined by "latitude"—distance from the equator. The equator is the imaginary line that runs horizontally around the earth and divides the northern hemisphere from the southern hemisphere. Distance from the equator affects climate because it means distance from the direct rays of the sun. That distance is measured in "degrees" of latitude—horizontal, parallel lines counted from the equator to the poles. (Similar imaginary lines of longitude run vertically from the North to the South Poles at fixed intervals around the globe. These lines are based on the Prime Meridian, which runs through Greenwich, England, and is the starting point for assigning time zones, but they are irrelevant to climate).

The degree of latitude shows how far a specific location is from the equator and from either the North or South Pole. With the equator as 0 degrees latitude, and the Poles as 90 degrees, either north or south latitude, the middle latitudes usually are the temperate zones, with warm summers, cool winters, and mild spring and fall. The tropics, closest to the equator (within about 0 to 22 degrees), are usually warm year around, with variations in wet and dry seasons, while the Arctic and Antarctic Circles are cold year round. Once air gets north or south of about 30 degrees latitude, it tends to cool and to lose its moisture.

Other elements can affect climate. "El Niño," for example, has received a lot of media attention in recent years. El Niño is the phenomenon of the Pacific Ocean warming along the equator, causing the trade winds to weaken and sometimes reverse, blowing west to east. This reversal allows warm tropical water to flow eastward to South America, increasing the temperature of the ocean there, causing water molecules to expand, and sea levels to rise. Since warmer water generally brings more evaporation, heavy rains fall over South America, which changes the atmospheric pressure and wind and rain patterns around the world.

Mountain ranges are another factor in precipitation. As air moving toward a mountain range is forced up by the rising land, it cools, condensing the water vapor it contains and creating rain or snow, so the area on the other side of the mountain is said to be in a "rain shadow," and receives very little rain, since by the time the air gets over the mountain, it has often lost its moisture.

Despite great variety in weather from year to year, the earth's climate has not changed much in recent history, although there is some controversy over global warming caused by burning fossil fuels. Over the long existence of the earth, climates used to be both warmer (shown by fossils found in the polar regions) and colder (ice ages). No one is sure what causes climatic change, but theories have ranged from meteorite collisions and volcanic eruptions (with dust and/or ash blocking sunlight) to the movements of the earth's plates or slight changes in the earth's tilt. Cloud cover can both absorb and reflect solar radiation, so clouds can have either effect of making the earth warmer or cooler. Much attention is currently being given to the possible effect of global warming as a result of the "greenhouse effect." The greenhouse effect is natural heating caused by gases in the atmosphere trapping heat, and it makes the earth warm enough to support life. The greenhouse effect does contribute to global warming, increasingly trapping more heat as the amount of gases, many of them from pollution, increase. A warmer earth might sound good to people living in cold climates, but warming oceans could melt ice, flooding coastal areas around the world, make living near the equator unbearably hot, and force plants and animals to adapt to warmer conditions or to die out.

READINGS FOR STUDENTS

Alexander, K. (1990). *The Kids' Book of Space Flight*. Philadelphia, PA: Running Press.

Apfel, N. (1996). *Orion, the Hunter*. New York: Clarion.

Asimov, I. (1991). *Ancient Astronomy*. New York: Dell.

Bendick, J. (1991a). *Artifical Satellites: Helpers in Space*. Brookfield, CT: Millbrook Press.

Bendick, J. (1991b). *Comets and Meteors: Visitors from Space*. Brookfield, CT: Millbrook Press.

Bond, P. (1999). *DK Guide to Space: A Photographic Journey Through the Universe*. New York: DK Publishing.

Branley, F. (2000). *The International Space Station*. New York: HarperCollins.

Branley, F. M. (1991). *The Big Dipper*. New York: HarperCollins.

Branely, F. M. (1987). *The Moon Seems to Change*. New York: Harper & Row.

Branley, F. M. (1987). *The Planets in our Solar System*. New York: Harper & Row.

Branley, F. M. (1987). *Rockets and Satellites*. New York: Harper & Row.

Branley, F. M. (1988). *The Sun, Our Nearest Star*. New York: Crowell.

Branley, F. M. (1986). *What Makes Day and Night*. New York: Harper & Row.

Burnham, R. (2000). *The Reader's Digest Children's Atlas of the Universe*. Westport, CT: Reader's Digest Children's Books.

Carle, E. (1996). *Little Cloud*. New York: Philomel.

Couper, H. and Henbest, N. (1998). *Big Bang: The Story of the Universe*. New York: DK Publishing.

Couper, H. and Henbest, N. (1997). *Black Holes*. New York: DK Publishing.

Couper, H. and Henbest, N. (1999). *DK Space Encyclopedia*. New York: DK Publishing.

Dyson, M. (1999). *Space Station Science: Life in Free Fall*. New York: Scholastic Reference.

Elsom, D. (1998). *Weather Explained: A Beginner's Guide to the Elements*. New York: Holt.

Flint, D. (1991). *Weather and Climate*. Danbury, CT: Franklin Watts.

Gibbons, G. (1987). *Weather Forecasting*. New York: Macmillan.

Harris, A. and Weissman, P. (1990). *The Great Voyager Adventure: A Guided Tour Through the Solar System*. New York: Messner.

Jackson, K. (1985). *The Planets*. Troll Associates.

Jay, M. (1987). *Planets*. Danbury, CT: Franklin Watts.

Kahl, J. (1997). *Weather Watch: Forecasting the Weather*. Minneapolis: Lerner.

Kelch, J. (1990). *Exploring the 60 Moons of Our Solar System*. New York: Messner.

Lauber, P. (1997). *Hurricanes: Earth's Mightiest Storms*. New York: Scholastic.

Locker, T. (2000). *Cloud Dance*. Parsippany, NJ: Silver Whistle/Harcourt.

Locker, T. (1998). *Water Dance*. San Diego: Harcourt Brace.

Ridpath, I. (1991). *Space*. Danbury, CT: Franklin Watts.

Seibert, P. (1999). *Discovering El Nino? How Fable and Fact Together Help Explain Weather*. Brookfield, CT: Millbrook.

Simon, S. (1998). *Lightning*. New York: Morrow Junior Books.

Simon, S. (1999). *Tornadoes*. New York: Morrow/HarperCollins.

Weimer, T. E. (1993) *Space Songs for Children*. Danbury, CT: Pearce-Everetts.

WEBSITES

California Space & Science Center's Teachers Resource Project
www.teachspace.org/

Space
kosmoi.com/space

Space Weather: Atmospheric Drag
www.windows.ucar.edu/spaceweather/sat_drag.html

Scientific Frontiers & Information Technology Homepage
www.itr.nsf.gov/sfit/

Day into Night
www.nsta.org/303

How Wind is Formed
www.stanwell.com/pdf/windCD_04.pdf

Living with a Star
sec.gsfc.nasa.gov/lws/lws_missions_sdo.htm

The Impact of Solar Activity on Life
canopy.lmsal.com/~schryver/Public/homepage/activityimpact.html

Edmonton Space & Science Centre
www.ee.ualberta.ca/essc/

Weather Influences
www.southpole.com/

Space Science News
SpaceScience.com

Earth, Space and Weather Science News
explorezone.com

Science & Space
dir.yahoo.com/Science/Space/

Science Museums and Exhibits
dir.yahoo.com/Science/Museums_and_Exhibits/

Web Earth Science for Teachers
www.usatoday.com/weather/wteach.htm

Weather Links/Resources
mcc.sws.uiuc.edu/html/links_K12education.htm

Teacher Resources
www.hprcc.unl.edu/nebraska/teachers.html

K–12 Outreach Using Unidata
www.unidata.ucar.edu/workshops/ShapingFuture/BestOtheWeb/
K12Unidata.htm

Meteorology for Children
weatherandkids.com/

Children's Science
www.ucar.edu/sciencestore/Children.htm

Science Links by Creativity Pool
www.creativitypool.com/science_knowledge.html

Junior Science
www.flexi.net.au/~willdown/state.html

Lightning
www.tmeg.com/esp/e_lightning/lightning.htm

Hydrologic Cycle Display
mac.usgs.gov/mac/visitors/html/exhibits/H2Ocycle.html

Resources
place.scholastic.com/magicschoolbus/theme/space.htm

Integrated Lesson Plans
faldo.atmos.uiuc.edu/WEATHER/weather.html

CHAPTER 7

THE PHYSICAL SCIENCES

MATTER

The physical sciences are chemistry and physics. They are integrally entwined, as they have to do with the physical elements and behavior of "matter," which makes up the world. Matter is anything that has mass and takes up space. Most of the emphasis in chemistry and physics is on non-living things, since living things usually are studied in biology. However, most of the precepts are applicable to living things as well, since they are also matter.

As early as 400 B.C., the ancient Greek Democritus theorized that any thing could be chopped into smaller and smaller pieces, until the pieces were so small they could be divided no more, a primitive version of the atomic theory. Democritus's idea was largely ignored until John Dalton, in the early 1800s, developed the atomic theory of matter: Dalton said atoms were too small to see, and that each type of matter was made of a different kind of atom. He even managed to split water into oxygen and hydrogen. But atoms have even smaller pieces—they are made up of electrons, protons, and neutrons.

It was J. J. Thomson who, in the late 1800s, discovered that neutrons are the negatively charged particles in atoms. A few years later Ernest Rutherford discovered protons, the positively charged particles in the nucleus, or center, of the atom, and James Chadwick identified the uncharged particles from the nucleus as "neutrons."

The number of protons in an atom determines the kind of matter something is. Protons and neutrons are held tightly together in an atom's nucleus at the center of the atom. Protons have a positive electric charge, electrons have a negative electric charge, and neutrons have no charge.

Electrons move around the nucleus in an "electron cloud." Electricity results from the moving electrons. Electromagnetic forces help hold the particles in an atom together. Electrons moving around the nucleus are held in the electron cloud by the pull of protons in the nucleus. But electrons also push each other away, as do protons, which are held in the nucleus by the "strong nuclear force," which is larger than the electromagnetic force pushing the protons apart.

In 1869 Dmitri Mendeleev, a Russian, grouped the sixty-three known elements by their properties. He put metals in one groups and non-metals in another, and he put them in order according to how much their atoms weighed. Mendeleev called his chart the "Periodic Table," and, with some adjustments, it is still in use today. Henry Moseley improved Mendeleev's table by arranging the elements by atomic number, the number of protons in the nucleus of the atom, rather than by atomic mass. The Periodic Table now has 112 elements, as Mendeleev left spaces where none of the elements known during his time fit.

In the table, each element has a block with the element's alphabetic symbol and two numbers. The top number, called the "atomic number," is the number of protons in the nucleus of an atom of the element, while the bottom number is the "atomic mass," which tells how heavy the atoms are compared with atoms of other elements. The "mass number" is the sum of the protons and neutrons, but occasionally, atoms of an element may have a different number of neutrons, and are known as "isotopes," to distinguish them from other atoms of the same element.

An element is a substance made up of only one kind of atom, and a period is a row of elements in the periodic table whose "properties," or characteristics, change gradually and predictably. The periodic table has eighteen columns of elements, each containing a group of elements with similar physical or chemical properties. It is also color coded to show metals, nonmetals, and metalloids—which share properties with both metals and nonmetals.

About three-quarters of all elements are metals, which are usually solid and shiny (the property of shininess is called "lustre"), and are good heat or electricity conductors. Other important properties of metals are "malleability," meaning they can be easily shaped, and "ductility," meaning they can be drawn out and formed into wires. Some metals are not pure, but are "alloys," mixtures of metals, such as bronze (copper and tin) or steel (iron and carbon). The second kind of element, nonmetals, are often gases or brittle solids, and, if solid, are dull rather than shiny, and are poor conductors, known as "inhibitors." Metalloids are solids that can be either shiny or dull, and can be either conductors or inhibitors.

Each element on the periodic table is represented by an element key, a box that contains the important information for the element.

This includes its name, its atomic number, its symbol (a one or two letter abbreviation usually, but not always, based on its name), its average atomic mass, and whether or it not it occurs naturally on earth or is synthetic (indicated by a bullseye). If it is a natural element, the indication shows whether it appears as a solid (indicated by a cube), a liquid (indicated by a drop), or a gas (indicated by a balloon) at room temperature. All the gases except hydrogen are on the right side of the table, and only bromine and mercury are liquids at room temperature.

An atom is the smallest unit of an element that has all the properties of that element. A "molecule" is two or more atoms linked together, and if they are linked only to atoms of the same kind, they are said to be in a "pure state." A "substance" is matter that has the same make-up and characteristics, called "properties," throughout. When pure substances, also known as elements, combine, they form a new kind of matter known as a "compound." A "compound" is a substance made of the atoms of two or more elements, such as water which contains hydrogen and oxygen. The compound is often very different from the separate elements that make it up. Adding the alphabetic symbols of elements together gives the name of the compound formed, and the proportions of the elements can change the compound.

The classic example is adding hydrogen and oxygen. In the proportion of two parts hydrogen to one part oxygen, the compound is called H_2O (water), but with two parts hydrogen and two parts oxygen, it is called H_2O_2 (hydrogen peroxide). The "law of definite proportions" says a compound is always made up of the same elements in the same proportion, i.e., water always will have two parts hydrogen to one part oxygen, and if those proportions change, it will no longer be water.

A "mixture" is two or more types of matter put together that does not combine to form a single new substance, as with water and rocks. In a "uniform mixture," the substance looks the same, although the two types remain separate, but in a "nonuniform mixture," such as a chicken pot pie, different parts still can be seen. When one material forms a "solution" with another, it dissolves. A "solution" mixes the particles of the different kinds of matter, although evaporation can separate some solutions, as when water evaporates and leaves salt behind in desalinization. "Solubility" is the measure of the amount of material that will dissolve in another material. For example, sugar dissolves in water but sand does not.

Although matter is usually either a solid, a liquid, or a gas, there is actually a fourth state of matter, called "plasma." Plasma is found in neon signs and lightning bolts, but most often in the upper atmosphere or in stars. These forms of solid, liquid, gas, or plasma, are known as "states of matter," and each has different physical properties, or characteristics. The physical properties of matter are color, size, temperature, smoothness or roughness (feel), reflectiveness, smell, fragility, bounce, stretch, and bendability.

Physical properties are often linked to the way matter forms. One important physical property is density, which compares the amount of matter to how much space it takes up. For example, a block of lead is said to be very dense, as it is much heavier than a same-sized block of some other matter. The amount of space matter takes up is called volume, and it is often measured in cubic centimeters. Mass is the amount of matter an object contains. Mass is measured in grams and kilograms, and standard measurements of mass are 50 grams, 200 grams, and 1 kilogram. The laws of conservation of mass and energy state that matter is never lost or gained, but recycled, with the same atoms, for example, of water, nitrogen, or carbon.

The ability of matter to float in a liquid or a gas is called "buoyancy." "Archimedes principle" states that when an object is placed in a fluid, the "buoyant force" is equal to the weight of the displaced fluid. The "buoyant force" is the net upward force caused by the displaced fluid. Basically, if an object's density is less than that of a fluid, it floats in the fluid, and if an object's density is greater than that of the fluid, it sinks. Air is less dense than water, so it makes bubbles as it rises in water. Helium, too, is less dense than air, so helium rises. Because an object will not float if it is denser than the fluid it is in, the oil in salad dressing, for example, floats on the vinegar, which is essentially water, but the bits of spices, onions, garlic, and parsley sink to the bottom of the bottle, because they are heavier than the fluid. If air is added, the matter becomes less dense, as with butter or a metal boat, both of which float when enough air is added. People float enough that divers need to wear weights.

Matter, as noted, is usually either a solid, a liquid, or a gas, and the particular arrangement of the particles gives matter certain properties. A solid has a definite shape and takes up a definite amount of space. A liquid is matter that takes the shape of its container. The amount of matter and the space matter takes up remain the same, though the shape may change. "Pascal's principle" is that pressure applied at any point to a confined fluid is transmitted unchanged throughout the fluid, which means if a person squeezes a flexible bottle, the pressure makes the contents shoot out. A gas has no definite shape and takes no definite amount of space. It spreads out to fill any container it is in, or to dissi-pate in the open air. Many things are part solid and part liquid, like fruit. Others, like water, can be solid, liquid, or gas.

Most matter can change physically through cutting, chopping, heating, cooling, etc. Heat, for example, can change things from solids to liquids, or even to gasses, through evaporation. When matter changes its size, shape, or form, it is known as a "physical change," because only the physical properties change, not the chemical ones. Matter can change size or change from one state to another, and the change can be done quickly or over thousands of years, as with weathering. A "reversible change" is matter that can be changed back to the way it was. An "irreversible change" is often caused by fire or cooking, such as a cake whose ingredients cannot be changed back.

Chemical change is more complex, because it happens when a substance or substances that make up the matter change into another substance or substances. Many useful items are produced by chemical change, including food, industrial items that are strengthened or weakened by chemical change, and chemical change is even apparent in such everyday occurrences as a bicycle rusting (the iron turning into iron oxide). Signs of chemical change are the formation of new substances, the giving off or taking in of energy, or color change. Chemical changes form different kinds of matter, as in cooking, burn-ing, and rusting.

A chemical property is a characteristic of a substance that allows it to change to a new substance. For example, milk can turn sour but it cannot catch fire, while a rock cannot do either. Acids and bases are ex-amples of liquids that have important physical and chemical proper-ties. Acids taste sour and react with certain metals or form acid rain. Acids may be useful, and they neutralize bases, but they can damage matter with which they come in contact. Bases have the physical prop-erties of tasting bitter and feeling slippery, but also have chemical prop-erties that can be damaging, and they neutralize acids. Acids and bases react with each other to form salts, such as table salt. The pH measure (commonly seen in testing swimming pool water) indicates the acidity, or lack thereof, of various solutions. A pH value of 7 is neutral, and be-low that is acidic, while above 7 is basic, and the farther from 7 in either direction, the more likely a solution is to be harmful. Another chemical property is "combustibility," which refers to how easily matter burns.

The rate of a chemical reaction can be different, depending on the temperature, on whether or not the mixture is stirred, or on the pres-ence or absence of a "catalyst"—a substance that changes the speed of a chemical reaction without any change to itself. The ability of a substance to react chemically is called "reactivity," and it may include a change in color, smell, or the production of light, heat, or gas. Sometimes it is hard to distinguish between chemical reaction and physical change, especially when chemical reaction causes physical change.

WAVES

Waves are regular motions that carry energy through matter or space, as when music is played on a compact disc and the sound waves travel. If matter (even air) is required as a "medium" to carry the energy, the waves are called "mechanical waves." Water waves are mechanical waves, because, despite the perception of the water moving forward, the water actually does not move forward, but, rather, moves up and down as the wave passes through it.

Another type of wave can travel through space and requires no matter—it is called an "electromagnetic wave." These waves are used for x-rays or to carry radio transmissions or television programs. If the matter moves back and forth at right angles to the direction the wave travels, the wave is called transverse, and if the matter moves in the same direction the wave travels, it is a compressional wave, such as a sound wave.

Waves have several other properties or characteristics. How high a water wave rises or falls above or below the water level is called the "amplitude," which is a measure of the energy the wave carries. The higher the amplitude, the higher the energy. Another property is the "wavelength," the distance between a point on one wave and an identical point on the next wave. The wavelength of light determines its color, as every color has a different wavelength. The "frequency" of a wave is its speed. Waves with longer wavelengths have lower frequencies, meaning fewer long waves pass a given point in one second. Frequency determines the pitch of a sound wave, and low frequency means a lower pitch, while high frequency means a higher pitch. In a thunderstorm, it is easy to realize that light (electromagnetic) waves travel faster than sound (mechanical) waves, since the lightning is seen before the thunder is heard.

Waves can reflect, such as light waves in a mirror or sound waves that cause an echo. They can also refract, or bend, when they move from one medium to another, such as from air to water, because the speed of a wave is different in different substances. "Diffraction" is also the bending of waves, but around a physical barrier, such as a wall. Sound waves diffract better than light waves. Sometimes waves overlap and form a new wave, a process called "interference." If the amplitudes, or heights, match up, they form a bigger wave ("constructive interference"), but if the altitudes don't match, the overlap forms a smaller wave ("destructive interference").

Sound is a series of waves from vibrations caused by things such as instruments, the throat, or branches rubbing together. Vibrations increase air pressure as they push, then decrease it as they pull. Sound waves are fast moving, alternating areas of high and low pressure. As they move, they spread out, so in a large area, sound is softer. Sound waves travel through air, water, and other matter.

In order for people to hear, sound waves hit the outer ear, which collects and guides them to the ear drum, which vibrates from the sound waves and moves the tiny bone at the outside end of the middle ear. Vibrations pass through three bones in the middle ear to the inner ear, which is shaped like a snail and filled with liquid. The ear walls are lined with tiny hairs connected to nerves. The third bone of the middle ear vibrates one end of the middle ear, causing waves in liquid, which move tiny hairs and nerve cells to send signals to the brain, which interprets them as sounds. Loudness is the measure of the amount of sound energy reaching ears.

"Pitch" refers to how high or low sound is, and pitch depends on how fast (high) the vibrations are. Thin string, for example, vibrates faster than thick string, and changing the thickness of a string makes it vibrate faster or slower, consequently changing the pitch. Additionally, the more the molecules are squeezed, the louder the sound, called "volume."

Sound waves move at different speeds through different materials. Denser objects carry sound energy farther and faster than less dense objects. The waves move faster through hard materials, as particles are closer together and bump into each other more often. Sound waves move slower through liquids and gases, but not all materials carry sound waves—there are conductors (wood, water) and insulators (cloth, styrofoam) for sound waves as well as for electricity. Because sound waves move through particles, sound waves cannot exist where there are no molecules of matter, as in outer space, which is silent because there is no air for sound waves to travel through. In air, sound travels about 1 mile in 5 seconds.

The reflection of a sound is called an "echo," and echoes reflect best from smooth, hard surfaces. Some planes, like the Concord, fly faster than sound. When it pushes sound waves ahead, then catches up, they are squeezed together and all their energy becomes one strong wave with a double boom, known as "sonic boom." Similarly, bullets fly faster than sound, so a rifle will make a loud crack when it is fired. To reduce noise, sound can be absorbed or spread out. Active Noise Control involves making the exact opposite of a particular noise wave, so the two waves' areas of high and low pressure cancel each other out.

As sound waves move forward, the molecules are squeezed together, a process known as "compression." After the first compression passes, the pressure on the molecules drops (called "rarefaction"). This process happens over and over if a sound is continuous.

ENERGY

Energy is the ability to cause change and is needed to move something from one place to another. The energy of motion is known as "kinetic energy," and any matter in motion has kinetic energy. The "kinetic theory of matter" describes the way particles move about. "Potential energy" is the energy an object has because of where it is or because of its condition. Potential energy can be "elastic potential energy," such as the energy stored in stretched rubber bands, while "gravitational potential energy" is the energy an object has when it is about to be acted on by gravity, such as the top part of a seesaw.

When an object's energy changes back and forth between kinetic and potential energy, it is called the "transformation of energy." The "law of conservation of energy" says energy can only be transformed—energy can't be created or destroyed. Some forms of kinetic energy are called "mechanical energy" and others are called "thermal energy" (the movement of molecules of matter produces heat) or "electric energy" (the movement of electrons produces electric energy). "Sound energy" moves sound waves to the ears.

Energy given off by the sun is called "solar energy," and it is a form of "chemical energy." It causes the seasons and is used by plants for photosynthesis, and by people and animals for various functions, including keeping warm and cooking. Solar energy exists in all living things, most of it stored in the chemical bonds that join atoms of carbon to each other and to atoms of other elements. Any material that can burn, such as wood, oil, natural gas, or coal, is called a fuel. The thermal energy in fossil fuels originally came from the sun as solar energy. When the original organisms were buried under sediments for long periods, the energy was buried as well, and that energy is converted to "thermal energy" by burning when the fossil fuels are taken from the ground ("biomass" refers to organic matter used for energy that is living or was recently alive, as with wood, peat, or even garbage). Unneeded thermal energy is called "waste heat." As the place thermal energy moves to becomes warmer, the place it moves from gets colder, which is one of the basic principles of air conditioning.

The energy that moves particles in matter is called "thermal energy," or heat, and it moves from one place to another in the particles in liquids and gases. Friction also causes heat, as do bacteria in compost. Thermal energy cooks food and heats water and houses. Temperature is a measure of the average energy of motion of the particle in matter— cooler particles move slower and vice versa. Two items can have the same temperature but have different amounts of thermal energy. Thermal energy is the total energy of motion of the particles in a piece of matter. When heat is added, thermal energy particles move faster.

"Conduction" is the transfer of thermal energy caused by particles of matter bumping into each other. Particles move faster as they are heated, and bump each other more often, transferring heat more quickly. Materials that allow thermal energy to move easily are called "conductors" and those that prevent it are called "insulators." Most metal conducts heat well, but other materials such as plastic and wood do not. A liquid thermometer works because when it heats, the particles move up the tube, and they move back down when it cools.

"Convection" occurs when a large group of particles in liquid or gases move from one place to another, transferring thermal energy which heats the air around it, forcing hot air up from cooler, dense air. Then the hot air cools and it sinks, and the process repeats itself. The sun's energy can not reach the earth by conduction or convection because there is no matter in space through which to move it, so the sun transfers bundles of energy that move through empty space by a process called "radiation," in which energy is emitted as waves, which includes light and infrared radiation.

Light energy gives colors, makes plants grow, makes cars move, and works on lasers. "Shadow" is blockage of light, and light bouncing off objects is "reflection." Light reflects off solids or liquids, or even gases. Light bends where two types of matter meet, a characteristic known as "refraction," but if the matter stops light, that is called "absorption."

Light is made of colors, and a prism breaks light down into its various colors. Light passing through a prism forms a rainbow. A drop of falling water acts like a prism when the sun is out and it rains, which is how rainbows occur. A prism breaks white light into colors, and it can mix colors to form other colors. Light not absorbed is reflected and is the color people actually see. Green grass, for example, absorbs all light except the green, which reflects back and the eye then sees green grass. Lenses have curved surfaces, which bend light waves in different ways, allowing different focus and magnification so people can better see things through telescopes or eyeglasses (according to Marco Polo, the Chinese had eyeglasses as early as 1275). Most light beams spread apart, but lasers focus the beam very narrowly so it can be used to cut information onto a disk, or carry messages along thin glass fibers called optical fibers. Lasers also are used in surgery.

"Electric energy" is electricity, and it is produced by the movement of electrons. Within an atom, electrons have a negative charge and protons have a positive charge, so the two opposite particles attract each other. Most objects have equal numbers of protons and electrons, and therefore no electric charge, but if electrons are attracted to the protons of another object and rub off, the object that has gained electrons has a negative electric charge (more negative electrons than positive protons) and the object that has lost electrons (and now has more positive protons than negative electrons) has a positive charge.

Space around an object where electric forces occur is called an "electric field." If an object has a charge, it then attracts objects with the opposite charge, and repels objects with the same charge. This attraction or repulsion is called "electric force," and its strength depends on distance—the closer the objects, the larger the electric force. Charged objects have potential electric energy, sometimes called "static electricity," because the electrons are not moving. When charged objects are close to each other, potential energy can become kinetic energy through the objects repelling or attracting each other. The flow of electrons is called "electric current," and once electrons have moved from one object to the other, the attraction is gone because the charges are balanced, thus lacking electric force.

Electric current is a constant flow of electrons, and to keep a current continuous, there must be a constant electric force, with a source of electrons such as that from a battery, dry cell, or generator. In the battery or dry cell, different metals in chemicals build up opposite charges. In the generator, invented by Michael Faraday in the 1800s, an outside force turns wires between two magnets into opposite charges. In either case, the opposite charges build up on the terminals, and electrons are attracted from one terminal to the other, so connecting the two terminals allows the electric current to flow between them. As noted with thermal energy, a conductor is any material, such as most metals, that conducts easily, while an insulator is a material that does not, such as rubber, glass, or wood. Resistors are materials that resist the flow of electricity but do not completely stop it, allowing electric energy to be changed into other forms, as with the filament of the light bulb.

The electric current is a flow of electric charges, and the path made of the current is called a "circuit." A circuit with only one path is a "series circuit." If the path is broken, no current moves through the circuit, as with cheap Christmas lights, which, when one bulb goes out, all go out. A "parallel circuit" has more than one path so if a path is broken, the current continues to flow (and the more expensive Christmas lights still light).

Electric current in a wire produces a "magnetic field" around the wire. A magnetic field is the space around a magnet where "magnetic force" acts. A magnet contains iron that attracts certain metals, usually iron and steel, and a magnet has two poles—places of strongest force (north and south). The two poles are the same, so each pole repels the other and attracts outside materials. If the wire is coiled around a core, it makes an "electromagnet." The magnetic field of an electromagnet is only temporary, as there has to be an electric current in the wire to make it work, and it can be turned on and off. The electromagnet can be made stronger or weaker with the addition or removal of coils of wire. Not only can electricity produce a magnetic field, but a magnetic field can produce electricity—if a coil of wire is moved near a magnet, current flows in the wire. A coil of wire, a magnet, and electricity are the basic elements of an electric motor. There are different strengths of magnets, and magnetic force can even exert itself through intervening objects. Because the earth is like a giant magnet, the magnetized needle in a compass points north, so it is easy to follow direction. It is thought that the Chinese were the first to use magnets as compasses.

FORCE AND GRAVITY

"Position" is an object's certain place or location. If the position is changing, the object is in motion. Motion is a change of position, also defined as movement from one place to another. Whether or not someone observes the motion depends on their "frame of reference"—they must be able to see the motion against a background which is not moving, in order to sense and describe motion. Motion based on frame of reference is called "relative motion." "Velocity," or speed, is a measure of an object's change in position during a unit of time. Speed is calculated by dividing the distance traveled by the time it took, to get the average speed. The rate at which speed or direction changes is known as "acceleration," which is found by dividing the change in speed by the time.

Force is needed to start an object moving, and that force depends on other forces acting on the object. Once an object is moving, it moves until another force, friction, stops it. Friction is a force that keeps objects that are touching each other from sliding past each other easily. The rougher a surface, the greater the friction. Friction is what makes brakes work. Friction makes it harder to move things: surfaces are different, some having more friction than others. Changing the surface by putting oil on machine parts, for example, will reduce friction,

Less force is needed to move light things than heavy ones, or to go a short distance than a far one. One can measure force by how far a thing moves or how long it takes. There are several different kinds of force, including inertia. "Inertia" denotes an object's ability to stay at rest. The more matter an object has, the harder it will be to move. Mass measures the quantity of matter, so mass also describes an object's inertia, but mass and weight are not the same thing, since weight can change, depending on the pull of gravity, but mass is always the same.

The force that pulls things toward the earth is called "gravity." Gravity is the attraction between all matter, stated in Isaac Newton's "law of universal gravitation," which says that all matter pulls on all other matter. Gravity, then, is a force that pulls all objects toward each other. How a force affects an object depends on the object's mass, because an object with more mass is affected less by force. The pull between objects with large mass is stronger than the pull between objects with small mass (the latter is usually unnoticeable). Usually the pull is not noticed, as small objects have small pull, but the gravity of the earth is apparent to everyone. The downward force of gravity toward the earth is called "weight." Weight is a measure of the pull, or force, of gravity on an object. On the moon, the weight of a thing would be only one-sixth as much as it is on earth, since the moon, being smaller, only has one-sixth as much pull. The greater the distance, the weaker the pull of gravity. Gravity is different on other planets, since they are all different sizes.

Newton also postulated other ideas or laws. He said that "an object at rest will remain at rest or an object moving straight at constant speed will continue this motion until an unbalanced force acts on it," as when a person is running and tries to stop suddenly. As noted above, friction, a force that resists motion, slows an object down ("negative acceleration"). In his second law of motion, Newton said that when an object feels a force, the more mass the object has, the harder it is to move it, so more mass means less acceleration. Newton's third law of motion states that forces occur in equal but opposite pairs, so that if a force is applied to an object, the object pushes back with equal force, as when someone walks on a road. Things ultimately move when the equal but opposite forces act on different objects.

The scientific meaning of "work" is the measure of force it takes to move an object a certain distance. "Positive work" is the term used when a force moves an object in the direction of the force, and "negative work" is the term used when the motion is opposite to the force, as when a ball is caught. Gravity can also "do work" on the ball, pulling it down. For "work," in the scientific sense, to be done, the object must move, and effort does not matter. In order to measure work, force is multiplied by distance. Power equals the work done divided by the time in which to do it.

Much work is accomplished by machines. There are six machines called "simple machines" that are the basis of most work. When two or more of the "simple machines" are combined, they form a "compound machine." The six simple machines are the lever, the pulley, the wheel and axle, the inclined plane, the wedge, and the screw.

1. A lever is a bar that turns around a point that does not move (called a "fulcrum"). When a person pushes or pulls the lever, he or she puts an "effort force" on one part of the bar, causing the lever to turn around the fulcrum, so the other end moves.
2. A pulley is a rope or chain and a wheel. When a person pulls one end of the rope, the wheel turns and the other end moves up. A "fixed pulley" stays in one place and is used on light weights. A "moveable pulley" can double force but needs to be pulled twice as far to do so. Pulleys can be combined to make elaborate "pulley systems."
3. A wheel and axle consists of a large wheel attached to a smaller wheel or rod, such as a doorknob. Effort force on a large wheel is made larger by force on the smaller wheel or axle connected to it.
4. An inclined plane machine is a flat surface with one end higher than the other. It changes the effort force through distance into a larger resulting force that lifts up the object. The steeper the ramp, the harder it is to slide a box, for example, so a longer, less

steep ramp makes it easier. However, friction is one problem of a long, inclined plane.

5. A screw is an inclined plane wrapped around a pole. The long ramp is wrapped into a space the same height as the plane, but with little width. A screw trades force for distance.

6. A wedge is two inclined planes placed back to back. As the wedge moves into a solid, the inclined planes are a force outward and to the sides, as with an ax head or knife.

All six simple machines help move things by changing the size of the force applied, the direction of the force, or both. For work to take place, the force and motion must be in the same direction. It is never possible to get more work out than is put in—for a small force to turn into a larger force, it must cover more distance, as when a light weight on the end of a see-saw moves a heavier weight closer to the center.

The six simple machines help people do work and are at the heart of most compound machines. A pair of scissors, for example, is a compound machine that consists of two wedges and two levers. Each blade is a wedge and a bolt that lets them move and turns them into levers.

READINGS FOR STUDENTS

Baines, R. (1985). *Light.* Troll Associates.

Berger, M. (1987). *Lights, Lenses, and Lasers.* New York: G. P. Putnam's Sons.

Berger, M. (1990). *Switch On, Switch Off.* New York: HarperCollins.

Bortz, F. (1996). *Catastrophe: Great Engineering Failure and Success.* New York: Scientific American.

Bradley, K. (2001). *Pop! A Book about Bubbles.* New York: HarperCollins Children's Books.

Brockel, R. (1986). *Experiments with Light.* New York: Children's Press.

Curlee, L. (2001). *Brooklyn Bridge.* New York: Atheneum.

Elsom, D. (1998). *Weather Explained: A Beginner's Guide to the Elements.* New York: Holt.

Fitzgerald, K. (1997). *The Story of Oxygen.* London: Franklin Watts/Grolier.

Gutnik, M. J. (1986). *Electricity: From Faraday to Solar Generators.* Danbury, CT: Franklin Watts.

Hecht, J. (1987). *Optics: Light for a New Age.* New York: Macmillan.

Jennings, T. (1990). *The Real Magnet Book.* New York: Scholastic Press.

Jennings, T. (1992). *Sound and Light.* Smithmark.

Lampton, C. (1991). *Sailboats, Flag Poles, Cranes: Using Pulleys as Simple Machines.* Brookfield, CT: Millbrook Press.

Pfeffer, W. (1996). *Marta's magnets.* Parsippany, NJ: Silver Burdett.

Romanek, T. (2001). *The Technology Book for Girls and Other Advanced Beings.* Toronto, Ontario: Kids Can Press.

Simon, S. (1998). *Lightning.* New York: Morrow Junior Books.

Skurzynski, G. (1997). *Waves: The Electromagnetic Universe.* Washington D.C.: National Geographic.

Taylor, B. (1991). *Batteries and Magnets.* Danbury, CT: Franklin Watts.

Taylor, B. (1990). *Bouncing and Bending Light.* Danbury, CT: Franklin Watts.

Taylor, B. (1990). *Electricity and Magnets.* Danbury, CT: Franklin Watts.

Taylor, B. (1990). *Force and Movement.* Danbury, CT: Franklin Watts.

Ward, A. (1991). *Experimenting with Magnetism.* Broomall, PA: Chelsea House.

Weiss, H. (1983). *Machines and How They Work.* New York: Harper and Row.

Wick, W. (1998). *A Drop of Water: A Book of Science and Wonder.* New York: Scholastic Press.

Zubrowski, B. (1991). *Blinkers and Buzzers.* New York: Morrow.

WEBSITES

Smithsonian Physical Sciences
www.si.edu/resource/faq/nmah/physics.htm

Lesson Plans
www.theteacherscorner.net/science/physical/index.htm

Resources
place.scholastic.com/magicschoolbus/theme/physical.htm

Activities
www.chem4kids.com

Periodic Table
chemicalelements.com

Activities, Demos
scifun.chem.wisc.edu/scifun.html

Physical Sciences Resources
www.psrc-online.org/

Physical Sciences
dbweb.liv.ac.uk/ltsnpsc/

Resources for the Physical Sciences
www.jisc.ac.uk/subject/physical/

University of Cambridge: School of Physical Sciences
www.cam.ac.uk/cambuniv/schools/physsci/

Energy, Science, and Technology Journal
pubsci.osti.gov/

Hands-on Activities
webpages.marshall.edu/~bady/RICK/CATEGOR. HTML

Science Task Force
www.sciencetaskforce.ie/

Online Physical Science Lessons
www.school-for-champions.com/science.htm

Physical Sciences Library
www.libraries.psu.edu/crsweb/physci/

Teacher Project in Physical Sciences
www.utsc.utoronto.ca/~admliaison/etped.htm

CHAPTER 8

SCIENCE AND TECHNOLOGY

Technology is the use of scientific knowledge to create tools or items people can use. Almost four hundred years ago, Francis Bacon, as noted earlier, unconsciously summed up the close relationship between science and technology when he wrote that, "Good science is useful science." Early humans invented simple technology such as the six "simple machines" long before humankind had grasped some of the most important scientific concepts, such as the workings of the solar system, the law of gravity, and atomic theory. Since the increased understanding of how the physical world works, there have been concomitantly increased sophisticated inventions.

Although the natural world existed long before both people and technology, the observations and data recorded from the time of the ancients, through increasingly careful scientific processes and habits of mind known as "the scientific method," has meant that the history of humankind has been in large part a history of ever more complex technology. Although the natural world is too big and too complex for the human mind to completely comprehend, once people recognized that many natural events occur in consistent, recognizable patterns, they could put that knowledge to use in figuring out how to induce certain events of their own volition. Many of the careful methods used in collecting natural scientific data are also applicable to solving problems and creating technology.

Technology, however, is only as good as the people who create and use it. As indicated in Chapter 2, technology is "value neutral," meaning that it can be used for good or evil. Wars, for example, have been so hideously effective at killing people in the last hundred years in part because of increasingly efficient technology. In the past, it was much more physically difficult and exhausting to kill an enemy in hand-to-hand combat than it is now to do with firearms or deliberate disease.

However, those who blame technology for humankind's ills are short-sighted, since often the very same technology can harm or help, depending on how it is used. Refusing to allow scientists to pursue knowledge to the best of their ability may mean never discovering possible ways to help people or to cure disease. It is further obvious that "standard of living" is often linked to the scientific advances of technology that save labor and save lives.

Technology has contributed to the "green revolution"—humankind's ability to grow exponentially more food to feed the hungry, and it has made contraceptives possible to help keep the population in check. It has also led to revolutions in medical treatment, transportation, and entertainment—notably through better satellite communications leading to widespread use of computers, cable television, and wireless phones. Even construction has been affected by technology, with the ability to build ever higher and bigger buildings, as well as the ability to destroy them.

A somewhat negative side to the technological advances of science is the problem of pollution. In the past, most pollutants were naturally occurring and could be naturally addressed or avoided, since the population was much smaller. However, widespread industrial waste and byproducts, combined with the geometric growth of the population, made possible through medical advances and the green revolution, means that disposing of harmful material such as nuclear waste, with its long-lasting radiation, is an increasing problem.

With all the advances and changes that technology has brought to the world, it is important to remember that neither technology nor science is static. Change is constant, and, as Alvin Toffler argues in his book *Future Shock,* the rate of change is ever-increasing, for better or for worse. Science has shown us that in the physical world there is on-going wearing down and building up, in addition to the changes contributed by humans.

There are many questions that science cannot answer, because it is limited to those things people can see or that give them a visible response to a particular stimulus. Science is the source of potential knowledge that can be tested by experiment, and accepted as truth or discarded partially or entirely, depending on how the experiment turns out. Interestingly, scientific truth is not always final, but changes as on-going experimentation makes new information continually available, showing why it is important for a scientist to keep an open mind.

Science and technology will never be completely finished nor completely known. It is, therefore, important that each person who wishes to understand and to make sense of his or her world have at least a basic understanding of the important concepts that shape that world. As technology has increasingly "shrunk" the world, making other areas more accessible through communication and travel, people have become more knowledgeable about other people and places. Clearly, there are inequities in how science is used and applied, with the so-called "industrial nations" usually in the forefront of innovation, but acquaintance with the important premises of the major sciences lays the foundation for every thinking citizen to operate competently in the larger world and to make reasoned and objective decisions based on whatever new knowledge humankind uncovers.

TECHNOLOGY AND TEACHING

The teaching of science has changed dramatically in one particular area in the past ten years—the use of technology. While content knowledge is paramount for teachers, delivery of that knowledge is very different than in the past. It is incumbent upon the teacher to learn to use the available technology, since science and technology are perfect partners in educating students.

Technology can include television, videos, videodiscs, DVDs, computers, computer-based instructional tools, computer software, CD-ROMs, and the Internet. Technology has become so integral to science education that the National Science Education Standards includes a separate standard with major emphasis for technology at each grade level. However, as with any tool, the teacher needs to choose the appropriate technology with the purpose of enhancing the learning of science, not just for the sake of using technology.

Teachers need to be able to successfully operate the technology of choice and be familiar with a wide range of resources to use with that tool. They should be able to critically evaluate the strengths and weaknesses of the technologies and resources they use, and to assess how well those two things relate to the science lessons being taught, keeping in mind subject matter, student diversity, and instructional strategies. Factors to be evaluated should include the knowledge and experience of the creators of the technological tool being used, the purpose and goals of the resource, the suitability for students, the utility for the science topic under study, connections to additional resources, and reviews by other educators.

Computers will probably be the most common technology in the elementary classroom. Teachers should be able to demonstrate the use of computers for problem-solving, data bases (including data collection and management), communications, presentations, and graphic utilities—while simultaneously applying current knowledge about instruction and assessments to the use of instructional technologies. Teachers also need to keep up to date on the educational uses of technologies, to enhance personal and profession productivity for themselves in addition to facilitating for their students.

Technological tools can be fun, but they should also be treated with respect. The ethical, legal, and equitable implications of technology should be reflected in the modeling of the appropriate use of technologies.

READINGS FOR STUDENTS

Adler, D. (1999). *How Tall, How Short, How Far Away.* Boston: Houghton Mifflin.

Bortz, F. (1996). *Catastrophe: Great Engineering Failure and Success.* New York: Scientific American.

Curlee, L. (2001). *Brooklyn Bridge.* New York: Atheneum Books for Young Readers.

Gates, P. (1996). *Nature Got There First: Inventions by Nature.* Boston: Kingfisher.

Macaulay, D. (2000). *Building Big.* Boston: Walter Lorraine Books/Houghton Mifflin.

McClafferty, C. (2001). *The Head Bone's Connected to the Neck Bone: The Weird, Wacky, and Wonderful X-Ray.* New York: Farrar, Straus and Giroux Books for Young Readers.

Romanek, T. (2001). *The Technology Book for Girls and other Advanced Beings.* Toronto, Ontario: Kids Can Press.

Selbert, P. (1999). *Discovering El Nino? How Fable and Fact Together Help Explain the Weather.* Brookfield, CT: Millbrook Press.

Simon, S. (2000). *Out of Sight: Pictures of Hidden Words.* San Francisco: SeaStar/North-South.

Skurzynski, K. (1997). *Waves: The Electromagnetic Universe.* Washington D.C.: National Geographic.

Thimmesh, C. (2000). *Girls Think of Everything: Stories of Ingenious Inventions by Women.* Boston: Houghton Mifflin.

Vanderwarker, P. (2001). *The Big Dig: Reshaping an American City.* Boston: Little, Brown.

Wilson, A. (1999). *How the Future Began: Communications.* New York: Kingfisher.

WEBSITES

Technology Integration
www.learning.com

Science News
www.msnbc.com/news/sciencefront.asp?0dm=20CT&cp1=1

List of Science Tech Websites
www.ala.org/parentspage/greatsites/science.html#b

Links to Resources and Activities
www.tamu-commerce.edu/coe/shed/espinoza/s/ellis-b-657.html

Teaching through Technology
start.miamisci.org/exchange.html
www.odedodea.edu/instruction/curriculum/science/sciencestandards/

Students on Nature of Science and Technology
standardssts/stsg2.htm

Gateway to Science and Technology
psci-com.org/uk/
www.cnn.com/TECH/ science and technology)

American Society for Information Science and Technology
www.asis.org/

National Science and Technology Week
www.nsf.gov/od/lpa/nstw/start.htm

Internet Science and Technology Fair
istf.ucf.edu/

Mathematics, Science & Technology Education
www.mste.uiuc.edu/

PBS TeacherSource—Science & Technology
www.pbs.org/teachersource/sci_tech.htm

Learning Science with Technology
www.sciencemaster.com/

Science and Technology Sites for Children
www.ala.org/parentspage/greatsites/science.html

Triangle Coalition for Science and Technology Education
www.triangle-coalition.org/

ScienceTrek
www.scitrek.org/

Teaching with Technology
nara.aist-nara.ac.jp/index-E.htm

A FINAL WORD

This book should help give teachers the impetus and the confidence to encourage their students' interest in science, and to teach the lessons that so often go untaught in the sciences at the elementary level. Whether the reason for the widespread neglect of science is lack of knowledge or interest on the teacher's part, or simply the pervasive time constraints of language arts, math, and "specials," science should be a part of the curriculum. Every child should have the opportunity to develop knowledge of the natural world, in earth and space science, biology, chemistry, and physics concepts, and of the influence science has had, and continues to have, on technology and on human society.

Clearly, there are omissions in this book—some deliberate because of space constraints, some inadvertent. The resource guide may help those who would like to pursue overlooked areas of study or further understand the topics discussed. Some of the information may be outdated before this book is published, but one of the joys of science is the wonderful torrent of new and continuous information. With the attention on the study of the humanities that began in the Renaissance, science began to thrive. Through the years, the sciences have covered many of the areas of most concern to humankind: advances in medicine and extending life; increased food production; the exploration of space; the invention of labor-saving machines; entertainment and communications innovations; increased warfare capacity; and new materials; and increased concern and attention to ecology.

Much of life is concerned with science, as it increasingly relates to and affects society and the individual, based on scientific discoveries and advances. This book aspires to help open that remarkable accumulation of knowledge to pique the interest and encourage the knowledge of the teacher, and through the teacher, to give the student the great gift of being a thinking participant in the scientific world.

GENERAL RESOURCES
FOR THE TEACHER

Note: Websites and student resources can be found at the end of each chapter.

There are many thousands of books, articles, and various other resources, including software and websites, appropriate for the elementary and middle school science teacher. From the plethora of materials available, there are some idiosyncratic favorites the teacher may deem helpful. The teacher will undoubtedly find many good selections well beyond our lists, particularly in the mushrooming websites, in the constant flow of new journal material, and in children's literature. There are also many good resources, scientific biographies, and general works easily found in libraries and media centers by particular subject name. In addition to the following general resources, specific suggestions are given at the end of each chapter.

The National Science Teachers Association (NSTA) (1840 Wilson Boulevard, Arlington, VA 22201-3000 and on the web at www. nsta.org) publishes the teacher-oriented journals, *Science and Children* (elementary), *Science Scope* (middle), *The Science Teacher* (secondary),and *Journal of College Science Teaching*, which contain helpful articles each month on teaching various science content. In addition to selling the various National Standards, NSTA also publishes and sells many valuable individual books and support materials that the teacher may find helpful. NSTA's web site at www.nsta.org has much valuable information about science teaching and many valuable links. Other journals with articles on innovative ways of teaching science content to elementary students are *Journal of Elementary Science Education, Journal of Science Teacher Education, Natural History, Science Activities, Science Education,* and *Science News.* Content journals for children include *National Geographic World, Odyssey, Ranger Rick's Nature Magazine, Scienceland, Science Weekly,* and *Contact.*

The elementary or middle school teacher who cares about content will find a classroom encyclopedia, either electronic or hardcopy, indispensable for answering the inevitable student questions on far-flung science material, and may also wish to acquire high school level textbooks as resources in the various content areas from the district school book depository. Dover Books (31 East 2nd Street, Mineola, NY 11501) and Bellerophon Books (36 Anacapa Street, Santa Barbara, CA 93101) are particularly fine resources for science-related coloring books and other similar materials. Scholastic Software & Multimedia (2931 East McCarty Street, Jefferson City, MO 65101), Sunburst Educational Software (Dept. EG53, 101 Castleton Street, P.O. Box 100, Pleasantville, NY 10570), Minnesota Educational Computing Corporation (MECC at 6160 Summit Drive North, Minneapolis, MN 55430), and Tom Snyder Productions (80 Coolidge Hill Road, Watertown, MA 02172), are among the leaders in producing science software, including constant updating of their older programs. Each January issue of *Science and Children* lists up-to-date resources for science catalogues and suppliers.

Comprehensive, descriptive, and analytic sources for children's literature relevant to science are posted on the NSTA website at www.nsta.org/404. Also helpful are C. M. and J. W. Butzow's *Science Through Children's Literature: An Integrated Approach* (Englewood, NJ: Teacher Ideas Press, 1989); the sixth edition of Donna Norton's *Through the Eyes of a Child: An Introduction to Children's Literature* (Upper Saddle River, NJ and Columbus, OH: Merrill-Prentice-Hall, 2001), especially Chapter 12 (Nonfiction: Biographies and Informational Books, which also present considerations in choosing nonfiction and science books); and Carl M. Tomlinson and Carol Lynch-Brown's *Essentials of Children's Literature,* second edition (Boston, MA: Allyn & Bacon, 1996), especially Chapter 9 (Nonfiction: Biography and Informational Books), with their attached lists of relevant children's books.

Good, general overviews can be found in many of the grade level or above textbooks: high school texts in particular are good, in-depth resources for the elementary teacher interested in a specific aspect of science: ninth grade earth and space science, tenth grade biology, eleventh grade chemistry, and twelfth grade physics are typical subject areas, in addition to electives such as ecology, anatomy, and astronomy.

GETTING STARTED EDUCATIONALLY

Abruscato, J. (1992). *Teaching Children Science.* Boston: Allyn & Bacon.

Althouse, R. (1988). *Investigating Science with Young Children.* New York: Teachers College Press.

American Association for the Advancement of Science. (1993). *Benchmarks for Science Literacy.* New York: Oxford University Press.

Bain, A., Richer, J., Weckman, J. and Redman, M. (1993). *Solomon Resource Guide: Science.* Vols. 1 and 2. Cincinnati: Solomon Publishing.

Barkman, R. (1991). *Coaching Science Stars: Pep Talk and Play Book for Real-world Problem solving.* Tucson: Zephyr Press.

Barman, C. (1990). *An Expanded View of the Learning Cycle: New Ideas about an Effective Teaching Strategy.* N. P.: Council for Elementary Science International Monograph and Occasional Paper Series.

Beane, D. (1988). *Mathematics and Science: Critical Filters for the Future of Minority Students.* Washington D.C.: The Mid-Atlantic Equity Center, The American University.

Blough, G. and Schwartz, J. (1990). *Elementary School Science and How to Teach It.* Fort Worth: Holt, Rinehart, and Winston.

Brandwein, P. and Passow, A. (Eds.). (1988). *Gifted Young in Science: Potential Through Performance.* Washington D.C.: National Science Teachers Association.

Bybee, R., Buchwald, C., and Crissman, S. (1989). *Science and Technology Education for the Elementary Years: Frameworks for Curriculum and Instruction.* Washington D.C.: The National Center for Improving Science Education.

Carin, A. (1993). *Guided Discovery Activities for Elementary School Science.* New York: Macmillan Publishing Company.

Carin, A. (1993). *Teaching Modern Science.* New York: Macmillan Publishing Company.

Charlesworth, R. and Lind, K. (1990). *Math and Science for Young Children.* Albany, NY: Delmar.

Dean, R., Dean, M., Gerlovich, J., and Spiglanin, V. (1993). *Safety in the Elementary Science Classroom.* Washington D.C.: National Science Teachers Association.

De Vito, A. (1989). *Creative Wellsprings for Science Teaching.* West Lafayette, IN: Creative Ventures.

Dobey, D., Beichner, R. and Raimond, S. (1998). *Essentials of Elementary Science.* Boston: Allyn & Bacon.

Doris, E. (1991). *Doing what Scientists Do: Children Learn to Investigate Their World.* Portsmouth, NH: Heinemann Educational Books.

Druger, M. (Ed.). (1988). *Science for the Fun of It: A Guide to Informal Science Education.* Washington D.C.: National Science Teachers Association.

Duckworth, E., Easley, J., Hawkins, D. and Henriques, A. (1990). *Science Education: A Minds-on Approach for the Elementary Years.* Hillsdale: Lawrence Eribaum Associates.

Elstgeest, J., Harlen, W., Jelly, S., et al. (1985). *Primary Science...Taking the Plunge: How to Teach Primary Science More Effectively.* Portsmouth, NH: Heinemann Educational Books.

Gega, P. (1994). *Concepts and Experiences in Elementary School Science.* New York: Macmillan Publishing Company.

Gega, P. (1994). *How to Teach Elementary School Science.* New York: Macmillan Publishing Company.

Gega, P. (1994). *Science in Elementary Education.* New York: Macmillan Publishing Company.

Hampton, C. H., Hampton, C. D., Kramer, D., et al. (1994). *Classroom Creature Culture: Algae to Anoles.* Arlington, VA: National Science Teachers Association.

Harlen, W. (1985). *Primary Science...Taking the Plunge: How to Teach Primary Science More Effectively.* Portsmouth, NH: Heinemann.

Harlen, W. and Jelly, S. (1990). *Developing Science in the Primary Classroom.* Portsmouth, NH: Heinemann Educational Books.

Haury, D. and Rillero, P. (1992). *Hands-on Approaches to Science Teaching: Questions and Answers from the Field and Research.* Columbus: Ohio State University.

Hein, G. and Price, S. (1994). *Active Assessment for Active Science: A Guide for Elementary School Teachers.* Portsmouth, NH: Heinemann.

Howe, A. and Jones, L. (1993). *Engaging Children in Science.* New York: Macmillan Publishing Company.

Kanis, I. and Yasso, W. (1995). *Earth Science Activities: A Guide to Effective Elementary School Science Teaching.* Boston: Allyn & Bacon.

Kneidel, S. (1993). *Creepy Crawlies and the Scientific Method: Over 100 Hands-on Science Experiments for Children.* Golden: Fulcrum Publishing.

Kramer, D. (1989). *Animals in the Classroom: Selection, Care, and Observations.* Menlo Park, CA: Addison-Wesley.

Loucks-Horsley, S., Kapitan, R., Carison, M., et al. (1990). *Elementary School Science for the '90s.* Alexandria, VA: Association for Supervision and Curriculum Development.

Meng, E. and Doran, R. (1993). *Improving Instruction and Learning Through Evaluation: Elementary School Science.* Columbus: ERIC Clearinghouse for Science, Mathematics, and Environmental Education.

National Center for Improving Science Education. (1994). *The Future of Science in the Elementary Schools: Educating Prospective Teachers.* San Francisco: Jossey-Bass Publishers.

National Center for Improving Science Education. (1989). *Getting Started: A Blueprint for Elementary School Science Education.* Washington D.C.: National Center for Improving Science Education.

National Research Council. (1995). *National Science Education Standards.* Washington D.C.: National Academy Press.

National Environmental Education and Training Foundation. (1994). *Getting Started: A Guide to Bringing Environmental Education into Your Classroom.* Ann Arbor, MI: Author.

National Science Teachers Association. (1993). *Science for all Cultures: A Collection of Articles from NSTA's Journals.* Arlington, VA: National Science Teachers Association.

Raizen, S., Audrey, J., Champagne, A., et al. (1989). *Assessment in Elementary School Science Education.* Washington D.C.: National Center for Improving Science Education.

Russell, H. (1990). *Ten-minute Field Trips: A Teacher's Guide to Using the Schoolgrounds for Environmental Studies.* Washington D.C.: National Science Teachers Association.

Saul, W. and Jagusch, S. (Eds.). (1992). *Vital Connections: Children, Science and Books.* Portsmouth, NH:: Heinemann.

Saul, W., Reardon, J., Schmidt, A., et al. (1993). *Science Workshop: A Whole Language Approach.* Portsmouth, NH:: Heinemann.

Scott, J. (Ed.). (1993). *Science and Language Links: Classroom Implications.* Portsmouth, NH: Heinemann.

Sutman, F., Allen, V. and Shoemaker, F. (1986). *Learning English Through Science: A Guide to Collaboration for Science Teachers, English Teachers, and Teachers of English as a Second Language.* Washington D.C.: National Science Teachers Association.

VanTassel-Baska, J., Bailey, J., Gallagher, S., and Fettig, M. (1993). *A Conceptual Overview of Science Education for High Ability Learners.* Williamsburg, VA: College of William and Mary, Center for Gifted Education.

Victor, E. and Kellough, R. (1993). *Science for the Elementary School.* New York: Macmillan.

Watts, M. (1991). *The Science of Problem-solving: A Practical Guide for Science Teachers.* Portsmouth, NH: Heinemann.

INDEX